MEN OF IRON
The Story of Cammell Laird Shipbuilders
1828-1991

by
D. Hollett

William Laird, founder of the yard.

CONTENTS

Front Cover:
The Cunard Liner Mauretania, built by Cammell Laird and launched at Birkenhead on July 24th 1938.

Back Cover:
Rob Roy, Laird ancestor.

First published 1992 by Countyvise Limited, 1 & 3 Grove Road, Rock Ferry, Birkenhead, Wirral, Merseyside L42 3XS, and Metropolitan Borough of Wirral, Central Library, Borough Road, Birkenhead, Wirral L41 2XB.

©D. Hollett 1992

ISBN 0 907768 48 2 Countyvise Limited.✗
ISBN 0 904582 12 4 Metropolitan Borough of Wirral Central Library.

*The Paddle Steamer, Manx Fairy, built by Lairds for the Ramsey Isle of Man Co. –
launched June 11th 1853.*

ACKNOWLEDGEMENTS

The author wishes to thank:

Mr A. J. Worthington, Director of Leisure Services and Tourism, Metropolitan Borough of Wirral, and Mr Howard J. Mortimer of this Department for their support in this venture.

Miss Marianne Laird, descendant of the founder of the firm, for granting me access to the extensive Laird Family Papers held by her.

Mr David Hillhouse, Mr Colin Simpson and Mr Philip Eastwood of the Williamson Art Gallery and Museum, Birkenhead, for the very great help and co-operation extended to me in this project.

Mr William Norton, Principal Librarian, for much general support in this project, and in particular for his help regarding the preparation and presentation of the many illustrations. Also Miss Carol Bidston and staff at Birkenhead Library for their support, help and co-operation.

Cammell Laird Shipbuilders Limited, and in particular, Mr D.J. Foulis, Director, Personnel & Employee Relations, Mr Frank Lindstrom, Mr Andrew Bowcock and J. Taylor.

Cunard Archives, Harold Cohen Library, Liverpool University for the illustrations of the *Mauretania*, etc.

My wife Vera, who gave much help and assistance whilst I was producing this book.

By the same author:

From Cumberland to Cape Horn – The Complete History of the Sailing Fleet of Thomas and John Brocklebank of Whitehaven and Liverpool, and the early history of their associated Company Robert and Henry Jefferson of Whitehaven, published by Fairplay Publications Limited, PO BOX 96, Coylsdem, Surrey CR3 2TE, 1984.

Fast Passage to Australia – The history of the Black Ball, Eagle, and White Star Lines of Australian packets, also published by Fairplay Publications.

Birkenhead and the Nineteenth Century Emigrant Trade to Australia, published in conjunction with the Australian Bicentennial Exhibition 1988, at the Williamson Art Gallery & Museum, Birkenhead, and published by the Metropolitan Borough of Wirral.

Royalties on the first 3,000 copies of this book are being donated by the author to :–

The Cockermouth Mountain Rescue Team, C/o The Hon. Treasurer, Mr Jim Hall, 9 Greenback Lane, Cockermouth, Cumbria.

The 315 ton paddle steamer, launched in March, 1852 – a passenger boat built for the Bridgewater Trustees.

Chapter 1

1828-1864

The world-famous shipbuilding yard of Cammell Laird & Company was established at Birkenhead in 1828 by the founder, William Laird. Since that date the yard has been responsible for the construction of over 1,400 vessels, which have varied in type and size from 50-ton lighters to ocean-going liners, such as the *Mauritania*, and from the early paddle steamer *Lady Lansdowne*, to the 23,000 ton battleship *Audacious*. In its heyday, this establishment, under William Laird and his sons, employed thousands of men, and was therefore foremost in the economic development of Birkenhead. The history of the Laird family enterprises though do not begin at Birkenhead in the nineteenth century, but in Scotland early in the eighteenth century.

The founder of the business in Scotland was Alexander Laird, thought to have been the son of a yeoman farmer from Kilmalcolm, Renfrewshire, just south of the Clyde. Born in 1715, probably at Port Glasgow, it was here that the young Alexander Laird established a rope and sail-cloth factory. The business must have developed rapidly for in 1736 he felt confident enough to open a branch at Greenock, and later took over a similar establishment started there in 1725 by Robert Donald. Little more is known about Alexander Laird, except that he married, and that his son John, who was to continue the business, was born at Greenock in 1751.

In the eighteenth century the demand for rope and sails was exceptional and the business continued to prosper. On March 26th 1774, John Laird married Janet Galbraith, the daughter of a ship's captain. The couple had a large family but sadly lost many of them while they were still very young. It was on February 14th 1780, however, that John and Janet Laird's third son William was born – the youngster destined to establish the great shipyard at Birkenhead. Young William and his brothers grew up in a loving, but strictly religious household, for the Lairds were devoted Presbyterians – noted for both their hospitality and piety. Life at the 'Glebe House', the substantial Laird family home, was never dull for more often than not it was crowded with fellow Presbyterians, or relatives. Dull it might not have been, but it was rarely exciting, except in 1794, when John Laird volunteered to join the Loyal Greenock volunteers, in answer to a threat of invasion by the French. At the same time he placed his vast sail loft at the disposal of the military for use as a hospital.

When he was fourteen years old, William Laird was sent to Glasgow to be tutored by the Revd. Mr Simpson, but his stay in the city was short for he returned home in 1795. The following year he was seriously ill with fever, but, unlike many of the Laird children he survived. Three years later, in 1798, with his brother Alexander, he was taken into partnership by his father, the firm then becoming John Laird & Sons. The Lairds were by now amongst the leading citizens of Greenock, other notable families being the Hamiltons, Galbraiths, and Forsythes, all of whom tended to live close to each other. Very much at the fringe of this middle class enclave lived a Captain Gregor Macgregor, who went by the name of Graham at times. (The Clan Macgregor, first proscribed by King David of Scotland about the year 1300, were still subject to this action at the close of the eighteenth century!)

Captain Macgregor, the commander of a ship in the West Indies trade, was considered to have done very well for himself by marrying Mary Hamilton. She was a daughter of Baillie John Hamilton, a leading citizen of the town, and direct descendant of the first Earl of Arran, and the famous Archbishop John Hamilton, whose life has been well recorded in Scottish history. Important to this story of the Laird family though is the fact that Gregor and Mary Macgregor had an exceptionally beautiful daughter named Agnes, which was soon to be noted by young William Laird.

In 1804 William Laird married Agnes Macgregor. It was a notable wedding so far as Laird family history is concerned, for Agnes Macgregor was the great granddaughter of no less a man than Robert Macgregor, commonly called Rob Roy – hero of Sir Walter Scott's famous novel, outlaw, one time major in the Jacobite cause, and leader of the still proscribed Clan Macgregor! Outlaw Rob may have been, but he was far more than that. He was a man of exceptional courage, good natured, and benevolent and humane, albeit in his own particular way. Agnes's grandfather was Rob's son Ronald who, with his brothers James and Robin, took their father's swashbuckling 'Robin Hood' lifestyle into the next generation but, alas, without their legendary father's finesse.

It was decided in 1810 that William and Agnes Laird should, in the interests of the business, move south to the booming port of Liverpool, with their three young children, John, Mary and Macgregor, where he was to set up a branch of the firm. Without delay he opened a rope works in the port, and also got involved in the sugar trade. In 1811 the Laird family were living in Bedford Street, while William ran his enterprise from an office in Hill Street. In 1813 he moved to St. James' Walk, remaining there until 1818, when he moved once more to Seel Street, this being his last address in Liverpool before he moved to Birkenhead.

To begin with business between the Laird enterprises in Scotland and Liverpool had been brisk, the apparent objective being for William Laird not only to open another works on Merseyside but also to obtain work for the factory in Greenock. By 1812 though John Laird began writing to William complaining at great length about the problems he was experiencing in obtaining good quality hemp, and the difficulty of finding ships to carry his manufactured rope and sails away from Greenock. John struggled on, but despite all efforts the firm finally folded in 1818. John Laird himself only survived this sad event by three years, dying in 1821.

As chance would have it, William Laird had arrived in Liverpool just three short years after the abolition of the slave trade. Whilst the slaves had suffered on the Liverpool vessels the port had prospered and expanded until by the year 1806 the number of houses in the parish of Liverpool alone amounted to 14,565. The population of the port exclusive of the suburbs was in the region of 105,000. The town of Liverpool was literally bursting at the seams, and so were the docks, with hundreds of ships from scores of nations cramming the dock system to capacity. Opposite, on the Wirral Peninsular, lay the then small settlement of Birkenhead, virtually undeveloped. William Laird was quick to spot the potential of this area.

In March 1824 William Laird arrived in Birkenhead. His mission was to buy-up land in Birkenhead from the Lord of the Manor, William Price of Bryh y Pys. A deal was soon concluded, William Laird becoming the owner of a large area of land on the edge of Wallasey Pool. On a portion of this land he soon set up a works to build boilers, and then, without much delay, a shipbuilding yard. Laird was now clearly a wealthy man, or at least one who was able to raise capital without much trouble, despite the recent failure of his father's business in Scotland. He soon involved himself, with Sir John Tobin and others in a grand scheme to drive a ship canal through Wallasey Pool to the mouth of the Dee. Laird and Tobin brought in the greatest engineers of the day, Telford, Robert Stevenson of Edinburgh, and Nimmo to vet, survey and cost the scheme, which they did enthusiastically, but nothing came of this particular venture. Undaunted, William Laird was soon involved in another great scheme related to the development of Birkenhead, the construction of Hamilton Square, named after his wife's famous maternal ancestors.

It was in 1826 that William Laird, and others, began to build Birkenhead's famous Hamilton Square, the plan of which was based upon a square in Edinburgh, designed by the famous Scottish architect, Gillespie Graham. Handsome though this great square was, and is today, its construction attracted criticism at the time. The view of some was that it occupied a very central site, which, in the natural course of development should have been occupied by shops. Although the Laird family were later to take up residence in Hamilton Square, the street in which his own house was built at this time was some distance away from the square, in Cathcart Street, named after one of the houses he lived in as a youth up in Greenock.

It was during the 1820s that William Laird had also become heavily involved in the shipping trade of Liverpool. In 1822 he established, with others, the St. George's Steam Packet Company, formed in order to run steamships between Liverpool and Glasgow – a truly revolutionary concept at the time. This company prospered and developed until it had vessels running from the principal ports in England to Dublin and Cork, and other ports in Ireland. The main claim to fame of this company was the fact that it owned the *Sirius*, the first steamship that crossed the Atlantic to New York, but in the 1820s this historic event still lay in the future. (The Leith-built *Sirius* made her maiden voyage in 1838; undertaking her great race across the Atlantic against Isambard Kingdom Brunel's *Great Western* in the same year.) The *Sirius*, it should be noted, was a wooden ship. But soon William Laird and his sons were to be foremost in the development of iron-built ships.

Two years after William Laird had started to build Hamilton Square, he took his son John into partnership, the firm now operating as William Laird and Son. Together they now began to focus their attention on the construction of iron vessels. The first they built was a 50-ton lighter, launched from their yard in October 1829. Two more similar vessels were launched from the same yard in 1832, and then, in November 1833 they shipped their first notable vessel, the famous *Lady Lansdowne*, a paddle steamer of 148 tons, built to the order of the City of Dublin Steam Packet Company. Unemployment was at this time rife in Ireland, and the need to alleviate it by developing navigation on the Shannon was being given top priority. This vessel was not launched by Lairds, but 'shipped'. This was because she would have been too large to have passed through the canal from Limerick so she was shipped out in sections, brought to Killaloe by canal-boat and assembled in the dock there. Today the remains of this historic vessel are still visible at Killaloe, where they lie in the river, a few hundred yards above the Lakeside Hotel's new marina. History was now being made in Ireland – and at Laird's yard back in Birkenhead.

News of Laird's expertise in the construction of iron vessels crossed the Atlantic. Impressed, a Mr Gazaway Bugg Lamar, a Savannah ship-owner, banker and cotton merchant, placed an order with Lairds for the construction of the *John Randolph*, a flat-bottomed boat of 249 tons intended for work on the Savannah River. Like the *Lady Lansdowne*, the *John Randolph* was to be built in sections and shipped out to her place of work for assembly on site. Under the supervision of Lamar's man, a Mr Scarborough of Savannah, the order was promptly executed. The various parts were duly carried on Captain Muir's barque, the *Alcyone*, which set sail from Liverpool with her precious cargo on February 5th 1834. She arrived in Savannah, after what must have been a rather rough passage on March 24th.

Whilst Laird and his men were busy in Birkenhead building this ship, Lamar was no less busy in America planning her importation into the country. In the 1830s there was what amounted to a prohibitory import duty of three cents per pound on imported iron products entering the United States. Unwilling to accept this situation, Lamar petitioned Congress for the remission of duty. In February 1834, whilst the ship was being sailed across the Atlantic in the *Alcyone*, Lamar's efforts met with success. Congress passed a special act authorising him "to import free of duty an iron steamboat with its machinery and appurtenances for the purpose of making an experiment of the aptitude of iron steamboats for the navigation of shallow waters".

Once at Savannah, the ship was received and put together in about twelve weeks. Although, as part of the contract, Laird had sent out five men to assist in her assembly, Lamar found that all the pieces had been so well made and marked that these men were not really required. With her engines made by Messrs Fawcett, Preston and Company of Liverpool, which were exported with the hull, this vessel gave many years of good service to Lamar.

Whilst William Laird and John Laird had been making shipbuilding history in Birkenhead, John's brother, Macgregor Laird, had been making history of another kind in Africa. Born at Greenock two years before the family had moved south to Liverpool, Macgregor had also been taken into partnership by his father, but soon relinquished this post. Macgregor Laird was a strong opponent of slavery, holding to the view that our whole attitude to Africa was wrong, as it amounted to little more than crude inhuman exploitation. Laird, being a sincere religious man, wanted to convert the African people to his Christian faith. He also wanted to develop trade with them, but unlike many he fervently wanted this to be done in a fair and honest manner. Motivated by these objectives, and inspired by the earlier expedition of Mungo Park to the dark continent, young Laird put all his funds into a proposed expedition mounted by the famed explorer Lander. The expedition, consisting of two steamers and a brig, sailed from Liverpool on July 19th 1832. The brig was the *Columbine*, which was to be placed at the mouth of the River Nun and act as a depot ship. The largest of the two steamers was the *Quorro* – a paddle steamer which had been built in just three months, the other smaller paddle steamer being the *Alberka* of 55 tons only. Designed by Laird himself, she attracted much ridicule and comment from the Liverpudlians, but she proved her worth by being the first iron vessel to make a long ocean voyage.

After overcoming many difficulties on the passage out, the three small ships eventually reached the mouth of the Niger. On October 19th 1832, Laird's twenty-fourth birthday, he took the *Quorra* and the *Columbine* across the bar, followed by Lander in the *Alberka*. Although Lander was in charge of the expedition, the vessels were so frequently separated on the way out that Laird, in the 'Quorra', after the death of her commander, Captain Harris, was left to a large extent to act on his own initiative. Many adventures, and much suffering lay ahead for this nineteenth century expedition. Lander himself was attacked by armed canoes when near the settlement of Angiama, and so seriously wounded that he died of the effects on February 2nd 1834. Macgregor Laird arrived back in Liverpool in 1834, with his health much impaired by the hardships he had endured. The whole adventure had been a commercial failure, but Lander had proved that the Niger was navigable for trade. For his pains Macgregor was elected a F.R.G.S. in London, and gave important evidence before the Parliamentary Commission on the navigation of the Indus in the year of his return.

Two years after returning from this expedition, Macgregor Laird became one of the promoters of the British and North American Steam Navigation Company, which was formed to run steamers from England to New York, the company being formed on June 2nd 1836.

The next vessel to be launched from the Laird yard was the 300-ton paddle steamer *Garryowen*, in September 1834. She was built to the order of the City of Dublin Steam Packet Company for work on the lower reaches of the River Shannon. She was well built for she gave thirty years service on the river before being sold for coastal work.

Two other notable vessels left the Laird yard in 1834, again, like earlier vessels, in sections, for construction on site. These were the *Euphrates* and the *Tigris*. This order brought a great deal of publicity to the Birkenhead yard for they were built to the order of the British Government and the Honorable East India Company for Major Chesney's famous Euphrates expedition. The purpose of this was to see if the Indian mail could be sent out by the Euphrates and the Persian Gulf – a somewhat shorter route out to the sub-continent than via the Red Sea. Disaster lay ahead though, for the *Tigris* was lost in a storm, and the *Euphrates* never managed to establish the new route. However, so far as Lairds were concerned, this was of secondary importance for the East India Company were deeply impressed by the way Laird had built his ships. As a consequence of which the East India Company soon became a very good customer.

Laird was now gaining something of a reputation for the construction of ships built in iron, a fact that did not escape the attention of a noted shipowner, Assheton Smith, who, in the spring of 1835, placed an order with Laird for the construction of an iron steam yacht. Friends of Smith, however, persuaded him that he had made a mistake. A yacht built of iron would never be safe. At first Smith wavered and then lost his nerve. In September he arrived at Laird's office and asked him if he would cancel the order. But the project was well advanced and clearly this was not reasonable, but, nevertheless, Laird agreed to comply with his influential customer's request. What exactly transpired between the two men is not recorded, but the circumstances of the case soon became known throughout the shipping and shipbuilding world. Smith had cancelled an order for an 'iron' vessel and by so doing strengthened the strong prejudice against the building of ships in this new material. In his own mind though, Smith was not really convinced that the advice he had obtained from friends about this matter was sound. In 1837 he made his way back to Lairds and negotiated with them to build another iron vessel.

The result of this deal was the construction of a very impressive 'yacht', the *Glow-worm* of 362 tons burthen, 150 feet long, fitted with a 100 horse-power engine. A fine yacht indeed, for at this time many merchant sailing ships designed for deep sea trading were much smaller than this! After being used as a yacht for some years, Smith did in fact sell her, and she was for many years a coastal trader, running between Scotland and Ireland. Laird had been wise in remaining loyal to Assheton Smith, no-one was credited with greater experience and discrimination in naval matters than this wealthy shipowner. His example, albeit a belated one, in putting his faith in iron ships, did much to convert others to its use.

Another famous ship was launched by Laird in 1837, the 188-ton paddle steamer *L'Egyptien*, which was the first iron steamer to make the long passage out from England to Alexandria, and thence up the Nile, where her arrival must have attracted much attention.

The captain of this ship was so pleased with his new command that he felt moved to write to Mr John Laird from Oporto on July 14th 1837, saying that he had arrived at the port the evening before, after a passage of just four days and twenty hours from Liverpool, despite a head wind and a heavy sea for most of the passage. Captain Clarkson was pleased to inform Laird that the vessel was an excellent sea-boat, "very dry and stiff". More importantly, he concluded that he had had no difficulty with the compass, which had been placed, according to Professor Barlow's directions, about seven feet above deck. David Wilson, engineer of the ship also wrote to John Laird, reporting that when the ship had been sent up the Nile, with Government dispatches, for the second time, one of the Pasha's admirals, and several other officers on board gave a most favourable report of her performance.

In October 1837 the yard launched the fourteenth vessel to be built by the firm, which was also the largest project they had undertaken to date. This ship had been built to the order of the General Steam

Navigation Company of London and was named the *Rainbow*, a vessel of 581 tons burthen. She was 185 feet long, 25 feet beam and was fitted out with engines of 180 horse-power. After being employed for some time on the run from London to Antwerp, the *Rainbow* ran for many years as a cargo steamer between Le Havre and London, and was only broken up in 1869. It is worth noting here that this Laird-built ship was the fastest of her day.

THE "ROBERT F. STOCKTON."

More maritime history was to be made by the firm, in conjunction with Ericsson and Captain Robert F. Stockton in 1838. At this time Ericsson was trying to persuade the British Government to adopt his plan for the screw propulsion of ships. Characteristically, he obtained no support from the politicians in London, so he fell in with an American naval officer, and businessman, Robert F. Stockton, who persuaded him to try his luck in the United States. The story goes that after one look at Ericsson's propeller he is said to have remarked: "I do not want the opinion of scientific men; what I have seen this day satisfies me." Stockton then showed his confidence in Ericsson by placing an order with Laird for the construction of a 33-ton vessel with an Ericsson screw propelled by a 50 horse-power engine. Launched at Birkenhead in June 1938 and named the *Robert F. Stockton*, she made a voyage from Liverpool to New York under canvas (her propeller having been taken out) with every success. Until the building of this vessel Lairds had only constructed paddle steamers; and it is correct to say that, with only one or two exceptions, she was the first screw vessel built. Once in the United States she was used as a propeller boat on the Delaware and Raritan Canal in which Stockton had an interest.

More work now began to come to the yard from the East India Company, who were more than pleased with other vessels built for them by the Lairds. In 1839 they placed orders for the construction of an armed flotilla to be employed in the defence of their interests in the East. Three vessels of light draught, and each carrying two 9-pounder swivels, were therefore built at Birkenhead for the navigation of the Tigris and the Euphrates. They were named respectively the *Nimrod*, the *Nitrocris* and the *Assyria*. They were all of 153-ton burthen and 103 feet in length, with a beam of 18 feet, and 6 feet 7 inches depth in the hold. Like other previous vessels built by the firm for the same company, they were sent out in sections and later put together by Birkenhead men, on the banks of the Euphrates. Orders for more larger East India Company vessels followed, but the most notable vessel the yard built for this company was undoubtedly the "devil ship" *Nemesis*.

![Nemesis destroying Chinese war junks, 1841]

Nemesis destroying Chinese war junks, 1841

The infamous Opium Wars had begun. British interests were seen to lie in 'opening up China to Western trade'. British merchants smuggled opium into China as a trade-off for tea. Not surprisingly, the rulers of China took exception to this development and the wars began. The *Nemesis* played a central role in the battles that followed her arrival in Chinese waters. She left the United Kingdom early in 1840 under the command of Captain, later Admiral, Sir William Hall, R.N., and although she was only a vessel of 5 foot draft, not designed for deep sea trading, the interesting experiment of sending her round the Cape to India was made. This was made possible by fitting the ship with a sliding keel and a drop rudder, and thus adapted, no real difficulties were experienced. At India she was diverted for use in Chinese waters and, amongst other things, blew up a fleet of Chinese junks at Ansons Bay, took part in the famous battle on the Bocca Tigris, and generally terrified the Chinese who dubbed her the "devil ship" and also offered 50,000 dollars in exchange for her – an offer that, needless to say, was not accepted.

In 1840 Laird built his first iron ship for the British Government, the 228-ton Mail Packet *Dover*. At last his persistence had been crowned with success. Prior to this he had spent years trying to over-come the prejudice of the Lords of The Admiralty, who stubbornly held to the view that iron built ships would never replace the "wooden walls" that had served Britain so well in the past. Thankfully the *Dover* gave excellent service (for over thirty years) which led to more Admiralty orders being placed, for the gun boats *Soudan*, *Albert* and *Wilberforce*, all of which were launched in 1840. The last vessel to be launched in this year was the 187-ton ferry boat *Nun*, which, in an unintended way, did much to promote the building of ships in iron. Two years after she was built, she grounded on the stone pier at Birkenhead, her stern resting on the pier and her bow on the bare rock, the distance between the points of support being 81 feet. The whole weight of her engines, 65 tons, was in the central section of the unsupported hull, but she was so well built that she floated off on the next tide without the slightest damage.

Business in 1841 was decidedly slack. Only one paddle steamer, the *Lady Flora Hastings* and two sailing vessels were launched, the first of these being the 270-ton sailing barque *John Laird*, which was built to the order of her master and owner, Captain St. Croix, who traded her from London. Sold in 1850 to Teighe and Company of London, she was traded to China by them under the command of Captain Case. She remained in the registers until 1856 when her commander was Captain J. Nash. The final fate of this ship, named after her famous builder, is unknown to me.

Despite everything, the Admiralty were still arguing that iron ships would never really replace wooden ones. At best they would only be suitable for work on rivers, or very short sea voyages. Perhaps because business had been notably slack at this time, or because Laird could stand this nonsense no longer, he decided to build an iron ship 'on spec' in a bold attempt to discredit their Lordships' arguments. The vessel in question was number 42. Laird no doubt favoured fitting her with a screw propeller, but as a concession to anti-screw prejudice, fitted her with the usual less efficient paddles. Soon after the keel was laid the Admiralty must have made it clear to Laird that they were not interested, but this did not upset Laird unduly for by now he had obtained the interest of the Mexican Government. The 788-ton man-o'-war now began to take shape as the *Guadaloupe*, which, fitted with 180 horse-power engines, two 68-pounders on pivots at each end, and four 32-pounder broadside guns was a most formidable fighting machine. At last, on the suggestion of Laird, the Admiralty sent down one of their first class surveyors to the yard to survey and report upon the ship before her departure for Mexico. The report was so satisfactory that the Admiralty requested Laird to send in designs and an estimate for a first class paddle-wheel man-o'-war, to carry the same armaments as the best fighting ship then built. The result of these negotiations led to the construction of vessel No. 51 – the famous *Birkenhead*. Built as a frigate, she was later converted for use as a troopship, because of the clamour the wooden-wall diehards raised about an iron ship serving as a man-o'-war. She sailed for Cork, where soldiers embarked for South East Africa. All went well until she had rounded the Cape when she struck a submerged rock. Whilst she was sinking the soldiers of the *Birkenhead* earned their immortality. Half naked and chilled by the night breeze, they willingly obeyed the order to 'stand fast' on the deck of the sinking trooper, in order to give the women and children a chance of survival. Most of these heroic men were drowned. The event took place off Cape Agulhas on February 25th 1852 but the memory of this act of self-sacrifice will endure for ever.

Another notable ship built by John Laird was the East India Company vessel *Loodhiana*, launched in December 1843. She was specially constructed with a shallow draught for river work, the river in question being the Indus. This great river rises in the mountains over 6,000 feet above sea level, and then flows for hundreds of miles on a ridge, high above the plains; while for 110 miles of its course it is a raging torrent. John Laird's *Loodhiana* was built to his own special plan taking into account these

Troopship Birkenhead

severe conditions. Once again Laird built well for the ship was found to answer so well that the only vessels subsequently constructed for the East India Company, for the navigation of the Indus, were built on the same principle.

Throughout the 1840s the yard continued to produce an amazing variety of vessels. These included the Mersey Ferry boat *Wirral*, and the 446-ton *Princess Clementine*, built to the order of the South Eastern Railway Company. Her sister ship the *Lord Warden*, built for the same owners being launched from the yard in February 1847. June 1847 saw the launch of H.M.S. *St. Columba* – a Holyhead Mail Packet, which was followed in January 1848 by a sister ship for the same service, the 716-ton *Cambria*. No ships were launched in 1849, but the following year four vessels were constructed and launched for the East India Company. Business was clearly now at a low ebb for July 1850 saw the launch of the 14-ton sailing yacht *Fidget*. During the year of 1851 many more small and insignificant orders were attended to, which included a 19-ton lighter, and a 55-ton screw vessel, the *Weaver*, built for the Weaver Navigation Company.

In the early 1850s, a change took place which would soon have a profound impact on shipbuilding in general, and iron shipbuilding, in particular. It was the removal of the Navigation Laws, which had been drawn up to protect our merchant fleet from foreign competition. These laws had specified that a large proportion of British goods had to be carried on British vessels – manned by a high proportion of British seamen. Thus protected not much radical thinking had gone into the design of vessels, with the result that many ships in the British fleet were below standard. Inevitably better ships had to be built, and as iron ships were by now proving themselves better than wooden ones, John Laird found himself well placed to benefit from this radical change. To compound matters Lloyd's of London finally acknowledged, in 1856, that iron merchantmen did exist by issuing specifications for them.

Throughout the early 1850s more and more vessels launched at the yard were screw, rather than paddle propelled. These included the *Forerunner*, built for the African Steam Navigation Company, launched in July 1852, the *Braziliera*, a larger vessel of 1022 tons burthen, built for the South American Company, launched on April 23rd 1853, and the *Lusitania*, also built for the South American Company, launched on August 9th 1853. 1854 was to see two very significant launches, these being the P & O ships *Nubia* and *Pera*.

The Crimean War of the mid-1850s was fought between Great Britain and France, as allies of Turkey, against Russia. In March 1854 the great allied fleets sailed into the Black Sea and bombarded Odessa. Subsequent naval battles in this war brought to light many design faults in British men-o'-war, all of which were of interest to, and had to be noted by, naval architects – and builders of war ships, such as Lairds. Accordingly, John Laird sent his second son John, then aged 20, to the Crimea to study the issue at first hand. The trip more than paid for itself for the knowledge young Laird gained led to the construction, for the British Admiralty, of what were known as mortar boats – craft of great strength and light draught.

The first of these vessels to be built at Birkenhead was the 102-ton *Cupid*, which was launched on November 13th 1855. The fact that she was launched on this date was something of a minor miracle, for work on her had only begun three weeks previously! Deeply impressed by the vessel, and Laird's ability to produce excellent ships so quickly, the Government promptly placed orders for a further sixty vessels of the same type. The contract for fifteen of these was given to Lairds, along with a further order for fourteen gunboats, each of 230-ton burthen. It was an emergency situation and John Laird was clearly out to prove that he and his skilled men were equal to the occasion. The whole order for the twenty-nine vessels was completed from start to finish in eight short months, at the rate of almost one per week, an amazing achievement. The gunboats were all constructed of wood, while the mortar boats were built of iron. All fifteen mortar boats were launched in the two months of March and April 1856, so as to be ready for the spring and summer campaign in the Baltic. However, a peace treaty was signed on March 30th, without advantage to either side, so one assumes the government found other uses for this formidable Laird-built flotilla!

Whilst 1854 had found John Laird junior in the Crimea, it found his uncle Macgregor busy with African related projects. Anxious to establish legitimate trade with Africa, he persistently advocated that policy as the best means of counteracting and undermining the evil trade in African slaves. With a government contract, he established the African Steamship Company, in order to trade on all parts of the west coast as far as Fernando Po. He also developed the idea of cutting off the trade in slaves by introducing industry into the interior, and developing the great river Niger as the highway of legitimate commerce with central Africa. With these objectives in mind he organised, in 1854, a trading and exploring expedition at his own cost and risk, although he did obtain some government help. The explorers ascended the river Tchadda in the steamer *Pleiad* 150 miles further than reached previously. Unlike his earlier expedition with Lander, not a single death occurred, because of a liberal use of quinine, and better equipment. All of this greatly encouraged Laird.

Laird's Graving Docks

Back in England he prevailed upon the government to enter into contracts for annual voyages up the river, for which purpose he built the steamers *Dayspring*, *Sunbeam* and *Rainbow*, and made repeated ascents with them. Laird pursued these undertakings with little or no prospect of personal advantage. Macgregor Laird's organised ventures to Africa resulted in a settlement called Lairdstown being established. They were also instrumental in bringing Doctor Livingstone to Birkenhead where he placed an order with the yard for his famous river steamer, the *Ma Robert* (the Africans' name for Mrs Livingstone). After his death in 1861 Elder Demsters took over his African Steam Navigation Company, and today his descendants live in New Zealand.

It was in the early 1850s that the Corporation of Liverpool were induced to look favourably on a scheme for the construction of graving docks, building ships, and workshops on land belonging to them south of Woodside Ferry. Messrs Laird & Company, together with Clayton & Co., and Messrs Clover & Co. entered into negotiations to open up their works on this site. The building work was started in 1854, and before December 1858, John Laird had moved all his extensive shipbuilding equipment from his old yard on the Great Float, Birkenhead, and from his Liverpool yard, in Sefton Street. Although this development was welcomed by Laird and his friends at Clayton and Clovers it was far from welcomed by other residents of Birkenhead. Up till this time the site, still occupied by the yard today, was filled with luxurious homes, most of which had delightful gardens running down to the banks of the Mersey. The respective residents put up a struggle to stop this development, but it was a losing battle – and the shipyard, sheds and railways came, and came to stay. The singing of the birds was replaced by the din of John Laird's "counter sinkers", "sledge hammers" and the thumping and clanging which go hand in hand with the construction of iron vessels. The new yard was a great improvement though for it had direct rail links with the Monk's Ferry Station, from which the railway linked up with other lines which even then ran to Chester, Birmingham, Manchester and Holyhead.

It was at Laird's shipyard during 1857 that work was started on Doctor Livingstone's famous river boat. This pretty little steam launch was built by order of the government to accompany the great explorer on his expedition to Africa. In consultation with Livingstone, but built under Macgregor Laird's patent, it was built in three sections, so that it could easily be transported out to Africa. Unlike other vessels at the time the hull and boiler were built of steel plates, which had been manufactured in Sheffield. Doctor Livingstone's proposed voyage up the Zambesi led to him giving John Laird a very difficult specification to work to, regarding weight, length (75 feet), performance and

Dr. Livingstone's steamer Ma Roberts

*John Laird,
founders son.*

draught. John Laird therefore decided to build in the new lighter material steel, the *Ma Robert* consequently having the distinction of being the first, or at least one of the first vessels to be built with this metal.

Soon the vessel was completed, and successful trials were carried out on the Mersey before she was broken down for shipment out to Africa on the screw-steamship *Pearl*. Once out in Africa though it was not long before trouble started. Doctor Livingstone was a stubborn man who refused to take the advice of his professional nautical colleagues, so far as the treatment of his small vessel was concerned. Despite pleas not to, he insisted on overloading the *Ma Robert*, and this to a degree that was bound to overstrain both her hull and engine. Another problem which neither Laird or Livingstone had allowed for was the effect that constant grounding would have on the thin steel plates of the hull. Heavy wear and tear soon led to serious erosion.

Livingstone, who tended to blame everyone but himself when things went wrong, wrote back to London blaming Laird for all that had transpired. The naval officer who had overseen the construction of the launch defended John Laird from Livingstone's accusations that he was a poor engineer, who had foisted a poor quality job on his expedition. Laird was after all only working to the specification put forward by Livingstone.

It was on January 27th 1861 that Macgregor Laird, lifelong opponent of slavery in Africa, died at the age of fifty-two. His brother John Laird also took the decision to hand over the management of the firm to his sons, for Birkenhead had just been made a parliamentary borough. John set his sights on Westminster, stood for the Conservatives, and was returned as the first member of Parliament for Birkenhead. He was to be re-elected at three subsequent elections. The firm now become known as William & John Laird & Company. The younger son Henry, already active in the firm in an executive capacity, was also soon admitted as a partner, the firm in 1863 becoming known as Laird Brothers. John Laird Jnr was soon to become known as the "hard man" of the firm. He had served a commercial apprenticeship with a firm of Brazilian merchants in Liverpool. After leaving this firm he had furthered his education by making a tour of France, in which country he studied what were then known as "Continental" business methods. What exactly these amounted to is left to the imagination, but conclusions could perhaps be drawn from the fact that his attitude to employees was afterwards marked by a streak of ruthlessness! John Laird Jnr though had a quick mind, and an alert eye for opportunity. It was said that he was not a speculator, but his approach to business was nothing if not adventurous, which no doubt would have been a contributory factor in events that were about to transpire regarding the firm, and the recently established Confederate States of America!

The third brother, Henry, shared his elder brother William's technical flair. He had been in the drawing office of a famous French shipbuilder. When he returned to Birkenhead he took charge of Laird's drawing office. Henry was noted for being a much more sympathetic man than his brother John, for when an employee was ill it would be Henry who made it his business to see that food and medicine were sent to the invalid's home. It was, however, Henry who was to sign a contract in 1861 that his deceased uncle Macgregor would certainly not have approved of. It was for vessel No. 290 – the ship that became the Confederate States raider *Alabama*. The signing of this controversial contract almost lost Great Britain the dominion of Canada, cost the Government £3 million, and without a doubt, John Laird senior any chance he might of had of being knighted! The American Civil War was now in progress, with President Abraham Lincoln of the United States fighting the break-away southern Confederate States of America. Work related to this deal was conducted in a manner which skirted round existing British neutrality laws, but this legalistic chicanery cut no ice with Abraham Lincoln or the Federal Government.

The Confederate agent James Bulloch arrived in Liverpool on June 4th 1861, significantly perhaps, just over four months after the death of Macgregor Laird. Under a cloak of secrecy he met with the Laird Brothers and soon persuaded them to build vessel No. 290. The contract was signed (by Henry Laird) on August 1st 1861. It was clear from the start that this screw steamer of some 1000 tons was no ordinary ship, for she was to be built to British Admiralty standards, with twin horizontal engines and at cost of £47,500. It soon became clear to all on Merseyside, and in particular to the United States Consul in Liverpool, who protested to the British Government, that Lairds were building a warship for the Confederate States of America.

Back in America at this time John Brown's spirit was on the march, as 185,000 negroes, most of them ex-slaves, were in the process of joining the Union Army to make war on the slave south, whilst

"The Birkenhead Drill"
Troops stand to attention on the deck of H.M.S. Birkenhead, as she sinks off the coast of Africa, February 25th, 1852. This heroic action enabled the women and children on board the vessel to be saved.

The Confederate Raider Alabama, launched on May 14th, 1862.

in Birkenhead, on May 14th 1862, the *Alabama*, alias the *Enrica*, was being launched by a lady thought to be Bulloch's wife. The ship slid down the Mersey soon after being fitted out, neatly dodging the United States warships moving in to block her escape, and made for the Azores. Here she was placed under the command of Captain Raphael Semmes, with Kell – owner of 100 slaves, acting as his second in command. For the next twenty months she cruised around the globe, sinking or capturing in all about sixty Union merchantmen, and thus playing a significant role in the less than noble cause for which she was built.

When the slave south finally lost the war the question of compensation by Great Britain for allowing the *Alabama* to be built on British soil was raised. A sum of 9 million pounds being considered appropriate. After much argument, accompanied by a veiled threat by America to occupy Canada if cash was not put on the table, it was finally agreed to put the matter before an international tribunal at Geneva, which, predictably found in favour of America, £3 million being handed over by Britain, a cheap enough price for Britain to pay in order to avoid war with the increasingly powerful United States of America. Meanwhile, back in London, the die-hard "wooden wall" enthusiasts at the Admiralty were finally routed, and in 1863 a full reconstruction programme was put into operation for the navy. Due to the *Alabama* affair, relations between Whitehall and Birkenhead were somewhat strained, so Laird only received a small part of this work. Well before the close of the century though all was to be forgiven, and orders for spectacular and innovative warships were placed with the yard.

Chapter 2

1865-1897

If vessel No. 290 was Laird's most controversial order, then vessel 321 for the Peruvian naval ship *Huascar* was surely the most notable. Laird-built ships are famous throughout the world, for being well built and staying in active service for many years. Few, however, can compare with Laird's oldest surviving ship, the 124-year-old iron-clad *Huascar*, maintained today by the Chilean Navy as a national memorial to Commander Arturo Pratt, who was killed on her deck in 1879 as he attempted to carry her by boarding. Lying proudly at her moorings in the Chilean naval base, her scars bear silent witness to broadsides fired at her in battles fought over a century ago.

Designed with the assistance of Captain Cowper Coles (famous as the designer of the ill-fated ship *Captain*), she was classed originally as a turret monitor; she was armed with two 10-inch guns in a revolving turret, of Coles' design, and a pair of 40-pounder shell guns. Her protection was formidable, consisting of armour plate 4.5-2.5 inches thick, all backed by 14 inches of solid teak. This 1101-ton ship was driven by a 1050 horse-power engine, which, with her single screw, gave her a maximum speed of 11 knots. Launched by Lairds on October 6th 1865, she was completed and sailed from the Mersey on January 17th 1866. Almost immediately though she became the centre of a diplomatic dispute. She put into Brest for stores and in order to recruit, but the French, after their experiences with the Americans during the Civil War, were touchy about their neutrality. Wishing to avoid similar arguments with Spain they detained the *Huascar* until hostilities ceased.

After arriving in America, little was heard of her for the next ten years or so, that is until May 1877 when the crew rose and declared against the Peruvian Government, whilst at the same time asking Chile to claim their ship. Having no desire to antagonise their neighbours, the Chileans declined this kind offer, all of which left the mutineers with only one option, to turn pirate. The *Huascar* now began a piratical cruise, levying contributions from passing merchantmen. Finally the British Rear Admiral de Horsey summoned her to surrender, but the pirate commander refused. The British ship *Shah* then fired a Whitehead torpedo at her, the first ever fired in action (which failed, however, to hit the *Huascar*). During the brisk engagement that followed the Laird-built ship was hit no less than sixty times, but only one 9-inch shell managed to penetrate her armour. Oddly though, the mutineers decided they had had enough, she steamed away and later surrendered quietly to the Peruvians.

Two years later, in March 1879, Peru and Bolivia were jointly involved in a dispute with Chile. The next six months featured a number of skirmishes between the ships of the opposing fleets, but on October 8th 1879, off Antofagasta, the Chilean cruisers got the better of the *Huascar* in a fierce and bloody battle, which ended when the Chileans boarded the Peruvian ship. She had been hit by twenty-seven heavy shells, but these had done only superficial damage to the Laird-built ship. It was the brave crew who had suffered, for thirty-eight of her company had been killed and more than forty wounded. It was through damage to her steering gear which led to her capture by the Chileans. More adventures lay ahead of this Birkenhead-built iron-clad, but she has remained in Chilean hands down to the present day, repainted in Victorian livery, with a black hull and yellow funnel – one of perhaps only two survivors of the iron-clad era, the other well-known one being the now restored British ship *Warrior*.

On November 24th 1866, just over twelve months after the launch of the *Huascar*, another naval ship was launched by Lairds, this being H.M. Transport *Euphrates* – one of the few government orders that the yard did manage to secure during this period – the other notable order being for the turret war steamer Captain. The launch of a great ship at Lairds was always a grand occasion, that for the 4,422-ton *Euphrates* being no exception to this rule. The ceremony of naming the ship was carried out by Miss Mends, daughter of Captain Mends, R.N., Director of the Transport Services. After the ceremony Messrs Laird's guests were taken round Isambard Kingdom Brunel's great ship – the *Great Eastern*, before being wined and dined in the new offices at the yard. Mr William Laird presided. The long speeches that followed were predictable. William Laird praised the government officers involved in the project, and they in turn praised Laird Brothers. All acknowledged that Government yards were better at building wooden ships than private contractors, and that some private yards were even poor at building iron ships, but Lairds could not be bettered in this respect! The *Euphrates* was one of the five ships then being built, under the inspection of the Admiralty, to carry on the improved Indian Relief Troops Service, by way of Alexandria and Suez. As the Suez Canal

"For King and Country"
Scene at the Laird Workshop – c.1914-18

H.M. Frigate "Birkenhead", 1846

The Captain in the Bay of Biscay.

was only started in 1859, and opened in November 1869 these vessels were certainly ahead of their time! However, the intention was to let two of these ships do the run to Alexandria, and another two do the run from Suez on to India, with the fifth vessel held in reserve.

The afore-mentioned turret war steamer *Captain*, a twin-screw vessel of 4,272 tons burthen was undocked at the yard on March 27th 1869. At precisely 10.00 am, a signal was given and the huge ship began to move out of the dock amidst a great deal of cheering from the thousands of excited spectators. They had much to cheer about for the ship was a remarkable one. Designed by Captain Coles, she was protected by one inch plate on her deck, but her gun turrets having armour plating no less than nine inches thick. Her main deck, however, was only eight feet above the water line, but on this was built a hurricane deck. Her screws were driven by 900 horse-power engines, all of which when related to the fact that her guns were built to 600-pounder specification, made her a most impressive ship. Alas though, she was ahead of her time, and as with so many prototypes was not to be a success. In fact disaster lay ahead for the ship, and her designer, Captain Coles.

On the evening of September 6th 1870 a squadron of H.M. ships were off Finisterre when a gale arose, and all square sail on the warships were taken in. Admiral Milne, on H.M. ship *Lord Warden* reported that the *Captain* was astern and closing under steam. At 1.15 am she was on the *Lord Warden's* lee quarter, about six points abaft of the beam. It was then that Milne noted that the *Captain* was heeling over a great deal. Soon after this it was thick with rain, and the light of the *Captain* was no longer visible. Eventually the sky cleared, and the stars came our bright and clear; the moon, which had given considerable light, was setting; but no large ship could be seen where the *Captain* had last been observed. When day broke only ten ships, instead of eleven could be observed, the missing one being the *Captain*. As the handful of survivors later confirmed the ship had heeled over and sank, with terrible loss of life.

In the early part of 1870 the National Steamship Company decided that they needed to add another vessel to their already considerable fleet. The result of this decision being the placing of an order with Laird Brothers for the construction of the *Spain*. This 4,512-ton screw steamer was launched at the yard on Tuesday, May 9th 1871. The ship was 437 feet long, and was fitted to carry twenty first class passengers and 1400 steerage passengers.

As an indication of just how advanced Laird Brothers were in methods of ship construction, it should be noted that the *Spain* had been built in one of their large building docks where the vessel had been under a permanent shed, protected from the weather, so that work could continue under all conditions. Another advantage of building in this dock, rather than on a slipway, was that the boilers and engines were fitted whilst the general construction of the vessel was in progress, and not at a later date, as was the normal practice. The engines of this ship were on the compound principle, and had also been built at the yard, under the superintendence of Mr Bevis, their Managing Engineer. It is also interesting to note that all the large forgings and castings, some of which were upwards of 25 tons were also made in Birkenhead, by George Bayliff of the Wirral Foundry; and the shafts by Messrs Clay, Inman & Co., of the Birkenhead Forge Company.

Amongst other vessels under construction at Lairds at this point in time were the screw steamers *Lusitania* of 3,008 tons, and 550 horse-power, the *Eten* of 1,800 tons, and 300 horse-power (built for the Pacific Steam Navigation Company), two steamers for the African Royal Mail Company, one of which was the *Yoruba* of 1,500 tons and 200 horse-power, and some barges to the order of a Mr Hugh Evans.

The fine steamship *Lusitania* was one of six of the same class then being built for the Pacific Steam Navigation Company, for their line from Liverpool to the West Coast of South America. As with the *Spain* she was built in a graving dock, under a permanent roof, and as she moved from her position on June 20th 1871 she was christened by Mrs Graves, wife of the M.P. for Liverpool. The famous Pacific Steam Navigation Company was in fact the first company to establish a direct Steam Line from the Birkenhead docks to any foreign port. Trade on this route was clearly brisk in the early 1870s for with this vessel it was the intention of the company to step up their departures from the docks from two to three times a month. Interestingly the *Lusitania* had accommodation for 132 first class passengers and 42 second class passengers on the main deck, and in addition space for 500 emigrants below decks. All of which clearly indicates that Latin America was now a very popular destination for the poor British emigrants seeking a better life far from home.

Another ship built at this time for the Pacific Steam Navigation Company was the *Santa Rosa*, a 300 foot long vessel of 2,129 tons. Again it was the intention of the owners to employ her principally on the run to Latin America. On this ship Lairds had built cabins for 106 first-class passengers and forty second-class. However, the space reserved for emigrants on the *Lusitania* had, in this ship been set aside for carrying cattle, in which there was apparently a large trade between the ports along the South American coast. How the accommodation for carrying cattle on this ship compared with that set aside for poor emigrants on the *Lusitania* I am unable to say, but one imagines there would be little to choose between them. This ship must have been a very unusual one, for in addition to her engines she was rigged as a three-masted fore-and-aft schooner, carrying large leg of mutton sails. These masts though also acted as derricks with steam winches, which could work simultaneously at the five large hatches. The *Santa Rosa* was launched at 12.30 pm on October 19th 1872. A measure of the importance of the occasion can be gauged by the fact that amongst the guests present for the ceremony were the Earl of Sefton, and Lord Garlies M.P.

The Birkenhead Ironworks was a remarkable place in 1874, with a series of five docks built specially for the construction or repair of vessels of every size. The largest of these docks was 440 feet long by 85 feet wide, docks number three and five being covered with what were described at the time as "elegant and substantial" roofs, both of which were specially arranged for the construction of iron-clad ships. The engineers', smiths', and joiners' shops ran for about 600 feet along Church Street. The Smithy in fact contained thirty-two fires in four rows of eight each. Here huge cranes were employed to lift the iron on to and off the hearths.

The boilermakers' shop was usually the most noisy part of the yard, the noise being so great that visitors were certain to get a headache just by passing through it. In the engineers' shop heavy machinery was to be found which was used to manipulate some 6 inch thick armour plating, used in the construction of men-o'-war vessels. On the north side of the largest graving dock was a 50 ton steam crane, used for lifting the engines and boilers into the vessels under construction. Amidst all this, steam trains clanked and rattled, carrying the huge sheets of metal used to build the ships, the line entering the yard through a tunnel, sweeping past the shops flanking Church Street, and going round by the sheds on the south side of the yard. Outside the entrance to the graving docks, between high and low water mark, was to be found a gridiron, which was used for overhauling steamers. It extended for a distance of 650 feet, and was built on solid rock.

So far as "Health and Safety" was concerned it is interesting to note that all the buildings in the yard were separated from each other by fireproof partitions. The men's dining room was 60 feet long by 30 feet wide, and was fitted with a large cooking range, which Laird's were proud to point out had taken a prize at the International Exhibition of 1851. On the walls of this dining room there were ranged little pigeon holes, each having a number painted under it. When a man wanted his dinner cooking he placed it in the pigeon hole (the number of which corresponded to his works number). The 'cook's' job was merely to heat what the men had brought in, placing it back later in the correct hole. Naturally this 'cook' was not employed directly by the firm, but by a committee of the work-men, the 'cook's' expenses being defrayed by a weekly subscription of 2d each, collected by those who made use of the room. The total number of men being employed by the works in 1874 being about 3,000. It was in this hive of activity in 1874 that two men-o'-war were built, the *El Plata* and the *Los Andes*.

The armour-clad turret ship *Los Andes*, built for the Government of the Argentine Confederation, was launched at Lairds' Ironworks on Thursday, October 29th 1874. This vessel, like her sister ship *El Plata*, launched on August 30th was of about 1,588 tons, and was propelled by twin screws, driven by compound engines, developing over 700 horse-power. This ship was very strongly built of iron, and was armour-plated from end to end. She carried one revolving turret, built to the system de-veloped by the late Captain Cowper Coles. Both these Argentinian ships had a shallow draught, for they were intended for the navigation of shallow inland waters and general coastal service.

The year of 1874 marked the passing of an historical era, so far as the shipbuilding town of Birken-head was concerned, for it was the year in which John Laird died. On the day of his funeral, all the shops in the town were closed and flags flew at half-mast. Thousands watched as his coffin was carried to Birkenhead Priory, with over 1,500 of his workers walking behind in silent respect. At a time when prominent industrialists could usually expect a knighthood, John Laird received no such honour, for Queen Victoria and the Government never forgave him for the disgrace the *Alabama* affair had brought.

In 1877 the 1,118-ton cross-channel vessel *Isabella* was launched. This paddle steamer was the first steel ship to be built by the yard, that is if we discount Doctor Livingstone's tiny vessel the *Ma Roberts*. Amongst other vessels launched in this year was the 1,512-ton sailing ship *Morna*, the 1,658-ton screw steamer *Thessaly*, and the twin-screw steel tug *Storm Cock* – the forerunner of a long line of Cock tugs built at the yard. 1877 also saw the handling of a Government order, H.M. tug *Sampson*, a paddle vessel of 300 tons.

In 1880 the firm built the *Lily* for the Holyhead to Dublin passenger service of the London & North Western Railway Company, with an identical sister ship, the *Violet*. Holyhead had been a passenger and mail port for Ireland since 1801, but communications between London and this Welsh port were much improved by the opening of a suspension bridge across the Menai Straits in 1826.

Until 1847, when the first railway-owned steamers appeared on the route, operated by the Chester & Holyhead Railway Company, the carriage of mails and passengers between Holyhead and Ireland was in the hands of the Admiralty; their sailing packets, and later steam packets, operating the ser-vice. In 1850 the crossing of the Menai Straits was improved again, this time by the opening of a tubular railway bridge. The year following this major development the Admiralty withdrew from the service and the carriage of Irish mails was put out to tender.

There were only two contestants for this profitable contract, one being the Chester & Holyhead Railway Company, the other, the City of Dublin Steam Packet Company. The latter managed to obtain the contract, but operated it in the face of stiff opposition from the railway company. 1880 was a notable year in the further development of the port of Holyhead, and the ferry service to Ireland; the inner harbour was opened by the Prince of Wales, and the L.N.W.R. started a night steamer service to Dublin.

It was for this service that Lairds had built the afore-mentioned *Lily* and *Violet*. Both were paddle steamers, 300 foot 6 inches long, with a beam of 33 feet and a burthen of 1,626 tons, the *Violet* being launched on February 14th, the *Lily* a month later on March 13th. For the time they were exceptional vessels; both could make the 70-mile crossing at an average speed of 16 knots.

By the end of the 1880s the L.N.W.R. decided to increase the speed of these twin ships, sending them back to Lairds to have new engines and boilers fitted. These magnificent vessels then continued to give excellent service until the *Lily* was withdrawn from service in 1900, and the *Violet* in 1902, by which time the L.N.W.R. had placed four new twin-screw steamers on this service. The famous old twins were sold to a company called the Liverpool & Douglas Steamers Ltd., which tried, without success, to compete against the Isle of Man Steam Packet Company. Both ships were broken up in 1903.

In 1882 Lairds completed their first order for the Cunard Line, the 5,517-ton passenger ship *Cephalonia*, which had the distinction of being the largest steamer built on Merseyside at that time. As with all early passenger liners, she did not rely on steam propulsion alone, being square-rigged on her foremast. However, her 4,000 horse-power engines did give her a speed of 14 knots. She had accommodation for 200 first class passengers and 500 in the steerage.

Order number 493 was also dealt with in 1882, this, significantly, being for a Government vessel, the 3,000-ton Indian troopship *Clive*, which was launched on November 15th. Another smaller Government order was completed and launched on January 13th 1883, vessel No. 506, H.M.S. *Albacore*, a screw-ship of 431 tons, and on September 1st 1883 H.M. paddle tug *Aetna* ran down the slipway. Other Government orders were soon to follow, clearly indicating that matters relating to the American Civil War were now a thing of the past.

Lairds were, and still are, noted for being able to produce any type of vessel, an unusual one being the 3,796-ton *Roman*, floated on September 20th 1884. She was built to the order of the British & North Atlantic Steam Navigation Company. As she left the dock she was named *Roman* by Mrs Yorke of Abergele, wife of a director of the shipping company. It is interesting to note that the vessel left the dock with steam up, her machinery having been previously fitted, something that was not possible when a ship was launched down the ordinary slipway. Once again Lairds efficiency was demonstrated by the creation of this vessel. The laying of the keel of this large ship was only taken in hand in September 1883. When she was floated just twelve months later she was practically ready for sea, only the masting and rigging still had to be fitted, which just took a further three weeks to complete.

What made the *Roman* unusual was the fact that she was built for the Atlantic Cattle Trade. She had specially-arranged cattle pens on the awning deck, as well as on the main and lower permanent decks, and had stalls for 1,100 beasts, with well-planned arrangements for watering, feeding and ventilation, whilst her winches were carefully built and arranged for the easy handling of her live cargo. She was fitted with a compound engine of 2,500 horse-power. The *Roman* was somewhat larger than the *Norseman* built by Messrs Lairds for the same owners two years previously, which had proved very well suited for the Atlantic cattle trade, having carried thousands of animals across the Western Ocean without many casualties, and with noted regularity and speed.

On May 12th 1885 another unusual ship was launched, the twin-screw cable ship *Britannia*, the first cable ship to be built at Birkenhead. She was built to the order of the Telegraph Construction & Maintenance Company Ltd. A 1,350-ton vessel, she was later to be bought by the Eastern Telegraph Company Ltd, which became Cable & Wireless Ltd. She remained in service for thirty-four years, laying and repairing cables around the East African Coast.

On September 11th 1886 the 524-ton, twin-screw H.M.S. *Rattlesnake* was launched at Birkenhead. She was the forerunner of a type of vessel considered by many nautical experts of the day to be of greater importance in naval warfare than the recently developed torpedo boats, an opinion borne out by the fact that there were already twenty-two of these vessels, then known as sharp-shooters, on the list of the British fleet. In engining these ships the paramount consideration had been to reduce weight to a minimum, consistent with efficiency. The propelling machinery of the *Rattlesnake* consisted of two sets of vertical triple-expansion three crank engines of 2,700 horse-power. The order for this ship was to be but the first of many for the Royal Navy, for between 1885 and 1900 four of the largest ships built for the Admiralty were built in the yard: the *Royal Oak*, 14,500 tons; the *Mars*, 14,900 tons; the *Glory*, 12,950 tons; and the *Exmouth* 14,000 tons. All of them had the largest reciprocating engines built for naval purposes at that time.

The 1,379-ton *Ibex* was launched at the yard on June 6th 1891, and promptly delivered to her owners, the Great Western Railway Company. She was built for the ferry service running then from Weymouth to Guernsey, which was at the time in great rivalry with another operator, the Southern Railway Company sailing from Southampton. At the time of her delivery the *Ibex* was the biggest vessel on the Channel Island service. She was also very fast, her triple expansion engines pushing her through the English Channel at over 19 knots. She quickly established herself as a very popular way of getting to the islands, for she was steam-heated throughout, and lit by the still novel electricity. The competition between the rival ferry operators was, in a very real sense, deadly, and almost led to the loss of the *Ibex* on April 16th 1897.

The ships of both fleets would often race each other in order to prove their superiority and it was during such a situation that the *Ibex* was nearly wrecked on the above date. She had left Guernsey just ten minutes ahead of the Southern ship *Frederica*, both vessels being bound for St. Helier. In a manner redolent of the great race between the *Nanchez* and the *Robert E. Lee* on the Mississippi, the stokers below decks sweated and toiled to maintain maximum power, whilst the respective masters did all in their power to outsail their opponent.

The *Frederica* was soon hard behind the *Ibex*, after just an hour's steaming, for she was a slightly faster vessel. On deck the excited passengers on the 'Ibex' cheered, as they looked back at their rival, who was by now only three cables behind. Both ships were abreast of Corbiere, where there was an inside passage through the treacherous Noirmontaise Reef.

Determined to win this race, Captain Le Feuvre of the *Ibex* decided to take a calculated risk, and take his ship through the passage. In order to do this the ship had to turn rapidly to port, and head back towards the *Frederica*, which manoeuvre must have surprised all, but the master of the Southern ship in particular! Both ships in fact just cleared, but after the turn Captain Le Feuvre became apprehensive about his proximity to the other vessel and altered course again. It was this second manoeuvre which brought the hull of the *Ibex* into contact with the jagged outer edge of the Noirmontaise Reef. Within seconds most of her propeller blades had been ripped off, and her hull punctured in two places. The ship though survived, but I cannot say if Captain Le Feuvre's career as a ship's master also stayed afloat following this incident.

On January 5th 1900, the *Ibex* was under the command of Captain Boudian. When approaching Guernsey he felt obliged to make a temporary alteration of course to starboard in order to get a bearing from the Casquets Light. Bad luck was with this commander of the *Ibex* also, for he brought the vessel too far over from the safe channel and, once again the hull of the *Ibex* found itself in contact with the unyielding edge of a jagged reef. The forward starboard bilge was torn open, and the ship began to sink rapidly, along with her captain's pride and prestige as a ship's commander. The thirty-four passengers were soon got into the boats, without loss of life. It was not until later, after a count was made, that it was realized that one member of the crew had lost his life in this accident.

The ship appeared to be in a good position to be salvaged, but the exceptionally strong tides here discouraged any English firm from taking on the job. At the end of the day it was the North Salvage Company of Hamburg which literally came to the rescue, working on a No Cure-No Pay basis. Eventually they managed to pass twelve 9.5 inch wire ropes under her hull, and, after some set-backs she was eventually lifted to the surface on July 24th. She was then taken back to Laird's yard where permanent repairs were effected and the opportunity was also taken to modernise the ship so that when she returned to service in 1901 she was virtually a new ship.

On February 8th 1892 *The Times* was reporting on the fact that there were two remarkable little iron-clads in Messrs Laird Brothers' Yard. They were the Argentine ships *Libertad* and *Independencia*. Recently-built by the yard for the Argentine Naval Commission, they were then being fitted out, prior to delivery. The specification for building these 2,132-ton ships had put the yard to a hard test. Amongst other things the Naval Commission demanded that each had to carry 340 tons of coal, have 8-inch compound belt armour along about sixty per cent of their hulls, have substantial bulkheads, one 8 inch, the other 6 inches thick, have an all round protective deck, partial double bottoms, and no less than forty separate watertight compartments! In addition, each had to be propelled by twin screws driven by compound engines of 2,780 horse-power, and be able to steam for four hours in a heavy swell at almost 15 knots. Each ship also had to be able to travel for 3,000 miles without refuelling, draw only 13 foot of water, and at that draft only displace 2,300 tons. Needless to say, Laird Brothers completed the order exactly as required. Whilst work had been in progress on these two orders, thousands of men had been working on a much more substantial one – vessel No. 579, H.M.S. *Royal Oak*.

On Saturday, November 5th 1892 thousands of people made their way from all parts of Merseyside towards the Birkenhead Iron Works, and other vantage points, such as the landing stages and river walls. They were gathering in force to witness the launching, or to be more precise, the 'floating' of the tenth and most powerful line of battleship to proudly bear the name *Royal Oak*. This was a day of

H.M.S. Royal Oak, 1894.

great importance in the history of shipbuilding at Birkenhead, and also a day conspicuous in the annals of the borough.

When all the notable guests had been accommodated on a platform erected around the bows of the 10.023-ton ship, the Lord's Prayer was read by the Bishop of Chester, Doctor Jayne, then the Psalm "They that go down to sea in ships" was sung. These formalities concluded, Lady Margaret Grosvenor broke a bottle of wine over her bows and christened her, following which she then attacked a silken cord with a small axe, which, by a complicated process let the vessel free. The *Royal Oak* was at once seen to move. A deafening cheer went up from the vast crowd, at which point the band of H.M.S. *Indefatigable* played the National Anthem promptly followed by the song "Off She Goes". The monster battleship then slowly and dramatically left the dock, under the tow of five powerful tugs – all of which prompted more cheering, and the firing of hundreds of rockets to mark the great occasion.

The *Royal Oak* was at this time one of the largest battleships constructed for the British Navy. She was one of the vessels built under the Naval Defence Act of 1889, which had laid down a plan for building about thirty-eight ships in Her Majesty's dockyards, and thirty-two ships by contract. With a crew of 800, four 67-ton guns, quick-firing guns on the broadside, and seven torpedo tubes, she emerged from Laird's dock on that November morning over a century ago as one of the most formidable battleships in the world. If that old Highland warrior Rob Roy Macgregor, ancestor of her builders, could have seen her, one wonders what his thoughts would have been. There is a tradition that when Rob Roy was on his death-bed he learned that a person, with whom he was at enmity, proposed to visit him. Hearing this, he asked that his great broadsword, dirk, and pistols should be placed by his side, so that it could never be said that a foeman had seen Rob Roy Macgregor defenceless and unarmed! With ships such as his descendants were now producing it was clear that Great Britain also had no intention of being seen defenceless and unarmed by her enemies! One suspects the old warrior would have been proud, but as he had mellowed a little in old age, perhaps just a little bit apprehensive also?

On a cold November morning in 1892, just two weeks after the launch of H.M.S. *Royal Oak*, a group of workmen began to lay the first of the frames for Laird's vessel No. 594. This was to be no ordinary passenger or cargo ship, but a 2,181-ton 'yacht', built to the order of the famous American millionaire, W. K. Vanderbilt! The *Valiant*, as she was to be named, was being built to replace Vanderbilt's yacht *Alva*, which had been sunk in a collision earlier in the year. Like the *Alva*, this replacement vessel was being built to a design by Mr St. Clare Byrnes, of Liverpool.

Almost unbelievably, just over four months later, on Wednesday, May 3rd 1893, the guests began to arrive at Laird Brothers' Yard to witness the launching of Mr Vanderbilt's 4,500 horse-power, brig-rigged 'yacht' – surely the ultimate thing in status symbols? The naming ceremony was performed by no less a person than Lady Alva Mary Montagu, daughter of her grace the Duchess of Manchester. Amongst those present were also the United States Consul: Mr T.H. Sherman, the Countess of Sefton and party, Lady Mainwaring and the designer of this remarkable vessel, Mr St. Clare Byrne and his wife. Ever thoughtful, Laird Brothers had seen to it that the launching bottle hurled firmly (but gracefully) at the vessel by Lady Alma, had been wrapped in the American colours. And, with even greater taste, they arranged for the American ensign to be hoisted at the fore – just as she took to the waters.

This vessel, which it was clearly a misnomer to call a yacht, had the dimensions of a fair-sized clipper ship employed on say the run to India by the Brocklebank Line, whilst her 4,500 horse-power engines were more powerful than those fitted to many iron-clad warships of the day! Alas, such was the price one had to pay if one wished to keep up socially with such as the Rockefellers, back in New York. 310 feet long, she had a beam of 39 feet 3 inches. The steel hull was sub-divided by watertight bulkheads, and she was fitted with a cellular bottom, arranged to carry water ballast. Teak had been used for upper decks and rail, and also for sheathing her deckhouse and bulwarks.

Her massive engines were capable of giving her a maximum speed of 17 knots, and to ensure that she did not run out of fuel, between social engagements, her bunkers were designed to carry 650 tons of coal! For the time she was an exceptionally modern vessel. She was fitted throughout with electric light, had two powerful searchlights, steam-powered steering, and a complete ice-making plant. Above decks the vessel was also very imposing, for instead of being rigged as a yacht, she was given a full brig rig, making her look even more like the afore-mentioned clipper! What this magnificent vessel cost I cannot say, but clearly it was a great deal.

Later in the same year Lairds launched two more warships, these being H.M.S. *Ferret* and H.M.S. *Lynx*. Known as torpedo boat destroyers, they were exceptionally fast and could be built, at least by Lairds, in just 100 days. Towards the end of the last century the firm was to complete no less than nineteen of them. Amongst vessels of this type launched the following year was H.M.S. *Banshee*, and H.M.S. *Contest*, both being 280-ton ships. 1894 also saw the launch of another yacht, this time though it was one of more modest dimensions than the one just completed for Vanderbilt – a 42-tonner, named the *More Vane*, built for the Duke of Westminster. Vessel No. 602, also launched in 1894, was one that did not attract a great deal of attention at her launch, or during her working life for that matter. She was the humble 143-ton barge *Penryn*, built to the order of the Liverpool Lighterage Company. Before this barge was launched work had already started on vessel No. 603, a Government order for one of the greatest battleships the world has ever seen H.M.S. *Mars*, which was to be floated some two years later, on the morning of Monday, March 30th 1896.

On this day, Mrs Laird, wife of the senior partner of the firm, had the honour of launching her Majesty's first class battleship *Mars*. At 14,900 tons she was an amazing vessel. 300 feet long, and with a beam of 75 feet, she was designed to sail at a maximum speed of 17.5 knots. Her motive power consisted of engines capable of generating 12,000 horse-power. The armaments of the *Mars* consisted of four 12-inch, 46-ton breach-loading wire-coiled guns, mounted on barbettes in pairs, which could fire a projectile weighing 850 pounds. In addition to these huge guns she had 50 quick-firing guns in all – twelve 6 inches on the main and upper decks, eighteen 12-pounders, twelve 3-pounder quick-firers, eight small machine guns (and five field guns).

The total weight of metal used in the construction of this huge vessel was over 10,000 tons. Another interesting feature of this battleship was her boats, which numbered eighteen, including two torpedo boats, which were stowed amidships. A strong steel derrick was fitted to the mainmast for lifting them and wood derricks were also fitted in the side of the casings for working the lighter boats. The ship was lit throughout by electricity, and also equipped with six searchlights of 30,000 candle power. Above decks there were two conning towers, fitted with voice pipes and telegraphs, to be used by the officers in charge of navigating the ship.

The officers and crew were accommodated on the main and belt decks, each officer having his own well-fitted cabin, with the senior officers accommodation being located on the main deck. The admiral's suite of rooms, which were very lavishly fitted out, as one might expect, were at the extreme aft end of the maindeck. Ventilation was taken care of by two large fans, 72 inches in diameter. The weight of the anchors and the chain cables was 112 tons, and if the cables had been laid out in a single line they would have extended for about a mile.

After the ceremony of naming the ship, five tugs towed the giant battleship out into the Mersey. Here she was greeted by the cheering of thousands of spectators, and the firing of numerous rockets. With the Royal Standard and Admiralty flags fluttering in the breeze she was towed slowly past the Birkenhead landing stages to the Great Float, her powerful appearance creating immense admiration as she passed by. The *Mars* was subsequently placed under the crane at the Float where she then received her masts, and the remainder of her armaments.

The history of the name *Mars* for British men-o'-war is an interesting one. It was actually taken from the French 243 years ago, when their 64-gun vessel of this name was captured by Captain Philip Saumares, of the *Nottingham*, in a battle at Cape Clear. Our captured *Mars* did nine years good service until she was wrecked when with the first expedition against Louisburg. The second *Mars* was launched two years later, saw service at Quiberon Bay with Hawke, and after serving on the active list for thirty years she ended her days as a hospital ship at Portsmouth. The third *Mars*, a 74-gun ship was launched in 1794. In the first year of her service she served as a rear ship with Cornwallis in the battle of Brest. At Trafalgar, with Admiral Lord Nelson, she was the third ship of Collingwood's line to get into action, and as history has recorded, served gallantly. She was eventually broken up in 1816. The fourth *Mars* was an 81-gun ship, which was built at Chatham in 1843. The great ship built by Lairds was therefore the fifth of her line. To mark the floating of this ship several attractive brooches were made and given to some of the ladies present, one of which is still in the possession of Miss Marianne Laird, descendant of William Laird, her builder.

All in all, the year of 1896 was a remarkable one in the history of Messrs Lairds, for as well as floating the *Mars*, they launched an entire fleet of ships for the City of Dublin Steam Packet Company. These being the *Ulster*, *Munster*, *Leinster* and *Connaught*, all of them identical 2,641-ton cross-channel steamers capable of just over 22 knots. The main function of these ships was to carry the Irish Mails. It was in 1882 that the Post Office had indicated to the City of Dublin Steam Packet Company that they intended to terminate their existing contract, whilst at the same time asking them

H.M.S. Mars, 1897.

22

to submit a new one based on vessels that could maintain a much faster service. After long negotiations, a deal was finally struck which resulted in the above ships being built by Laird Brothers for the firm.

All of these ships were built to a very high standard. The *Leinster*, typical of all four ships, was launched on October 21st. Her hull was built of steel, and there were ten watertight compartments so designed that even if the two largest of these should have filled with water the vessel would still have been in a safe condition. She had two pole masts, and two funnels, and a flush deck on which were located three deckhouses. The first-class dining saloon was described as a 'noble apartment', 40 feet long and 24 feet broad, extending the full width of the ship, capable of dining about eighty passengers at each sitting. The furnishings had been entrusted to Messrs Waring & Sons Ltd, of Liverpool, who had seen to it that the ladies' deck saloon was fitted out in Louis XVI style, with the dining saloon being Sheraton style in mahogany. Once again Lairds demonstrated their thoughtfulness by seeing to it that all the lavatories were fitted with Utley's patent ventilating side-lights. These were specially designed so that they could be kept open in bad weather – no doubt a prime consideration on cross-channel vessels, on which much eating and drinking was the rule, and rough passages extremely frequent!

As will have been noted, Laird Brothers had by now built many ships for foreign navies, particularly those of South America. In 1897 they launched the training ship *President Sarmiento* for the Argentine Navy. Named after President Domingo Faustino Sarmiento, the man responsible for establishing the Argentine Naval Academy, she is a remarkable ship. Although built of steel, she was wood-sheathed and coppered below the water-line. She was fitted with two engines, one a Niclausse, the other a Yarrow, which developed 2,800 horse-power, giving her a speed of 15 knots.

Despite the fact that she was only a training ship, she was remarkably well armed for she carried three 4.5 inch guns, one 4 inch gun, two 6-pounders and two 3-pounders. In addition to all these guns, she was also fitted with three torpedo tubes! She proudly represented her country on many occasions, having shown her nation's flag at such grand occasions as the Coronation of King Edward V, and also the inauguration of President Taft of the United States. The average distance covered on her training cruises was about 20,000 miles, but on her first cruise, which was not her longest, she sailed some 50,000 miles, which took her right round the globe.

Presidente Sarmiento

In 1925 she was returned to Lairds at Birkenhead for a complete overhaul, and modernisation. After this refit she returned to service once more, making a further fourteen notable training cruises, before becoming a stationary school ship. By this time this soundly-built Birkenhead vessel had won a warm place in the hearts of all Argentinians, to the extent that various plans put forward from time to time to have her scrapped soon met with this fate themselves. Today, almost a century later, this great ship is still afloat and serving as a schoolship for cadets of the Naval Academy.

The 12613 ton passenger and meat vessel Almeda, built for the Blue Star Line and launched on 21st September 1926.

Chapter 3
1897-1937

During the closing years of the last century Lairds produced many ships for the Royal Navy, these included the Motor Torpedo Boats, H.M.S. *Ernest, Griffon, Panther, Seal* and *Wolf*, all of which were launched in 1896 and 1897. In 1899 yet another spectacular battleship was launched, this being the 12,950-ton H.M.S. *Glory*. Ever versatile, the yard then accepted an order from the Prince of Monaco, this being to build his 1,368-ton yacht *Princess Alice*. Order No. 638 was for the 14,000-ton battleship *Exmouth*, which was built in the largest dry dock, the length of which was only 440 feet. Floated on August 31st 1901 her construction had spotlighted a problem now faced by the yard, for the dock was too small to accommodate *Exmouth's* mighty ram bow, and consequently had to be extended.

It was now clear that the demand was for larger ships, both naval and merchant, and that the yard was no longer capable of handling such orders, without much larger docks. The only way forward was to acquire more land. This was only available on the south side of the premises. Here were located a row of imposing private houses, a small shipyard owned by Messrs John Jones & Sons, and the premises of the Royal Mersey Yacht Club. A deal was struck with Jones & Sons, and the yachting fraternity, and private residents were moved out, but, as might be imagined, not without putting up some resistance.

The result of the afore-mentioned developments were that the total area of the yard now extended to some ninety-nine acres. On this vast new site six new slipways were laid down, the biggest being designed to take a ship 1,000 feet long. Graving Docks number 6 and 7 were built and the excavated material used for land reclamation. Impressive new boiler·and engine sheds were built, and to improve internal transportation of heavy items, a completely new rail system was built. The 15-acre fitting-out basin became the largest private wet dock in Britain.

This period also saw structural changes in management. The brothers William, John and Henry Laird had all died before the turn of the century. In 1899 Laird Brothers had become Laird Brothers Ltd.

H.M.S. Glory

The new limited company now having at the helm J. Macgregor Laird (son of John, and senior partner), Roy M. Laird and J.W.P. Laird. In 1903 the firm amalgamated with Charles Cammell & Co. Ltd., the Sheffield steel makers, to become Cammell Laird & Company Limited.

The world-famous firm of Charles Cammell & Company Limited was a very large producer of high quality steel. Charles Cammell, a native of Hull, made his way to Sheffield, setting up his steel business there in 1828. By coincidence at about the same time William Laird was establishing his business in Birkenhead! Charles Cammell's business moved forward with the development of the railway system, for his company supplied many of the rails. It was in 1861 though that he began to diversify in a significant way, this by experimenting in the production of heavy armour plating for ships. Soon this became their main product, and for some years before the merger Lairds had bought most of their armour plating from Cammell.

At the time of the Cammell and Laird merger, the former enterprise was already a vast one, part owning an ordnance works at Coventry, Cumbrian iron ore and coal mines, and a huge smelting works on the banks of the Solway Firth at Workington. In Imperial, pre-revolutionary Russia, they owned a file factory at Odessa. Cammell was also the outright owner of the Grimesthorpe and the Cyclops steel works in Sheffield, and another iron works at Penistone. This powerful new company elected John MacGregor Laird to act as Chairman.

The reconstruction programme was now well in hand, but the cost of this development must have been enormous, putting a strain on the resources even of this huge new amalgamated enterprise. For the first years of the twentieth century the firm made losses, but the company struggled on until by 1909 it began to show a profit once more.

From the Laird shipyard in 1909 there also emerged the Mersey Docks and Harbour Board's giant dredger *Leviathan*, the biggest dredger in the world! She carried accommodation for a crew of forty-four, had twin screws, and was powered by a pair of giant triple expansion engines. On Merseyside this vessel soon became affectionately known as the "Levi" and the "Scowse Boat". Each working day this vessel was capable of filling herself with 40,000 tons of sand, for she could make four trips out of the Mersey within the twenty-four hours, each time laden with 10,000 tons, which she was capable of lifting from a maximum depth of 70 feet – loading each time in about fifty minutes.

Leviathan

To keep the giant vessel on the move at all times the ship had four captains. On board at any given time there were two complete crews; and on shore, there were two more complete crews. They worked on a week on/week off system, which seems an enviable arrangement, giving each crew every other week off duty, but it has to be borne in mind that whilst on duty each man had to put in an eighty-four hour week, serving on alternate four-hourly watches. This remarkable vessel remained in service until well after the conclusion of the Second World War.

Other notable launches included the 7,117-ton *Highland Laddie*, built to the order of the Nelson Steam Navigation Company. She was a passenger ship, but one that was also especially adapted for the carriage of frozen meat. Other similar ships for this firm were launched in 1910 and 1911, the *Highland Brae*, the *Highland Loch* and the *Highland Piper*.

The morning tide on the Mersey on August 14th 1912 was an exceptionally high one, and therefore particularly suited to what was timed to occur at 11.30 am, namely the floating of one of the most remarkable vessels ever built by Cammell Laird & Company, a 49,000-ton floating dock, the largest in the world, built for the Admiralty for naval work at Portsmouth. Shortly after the above time a number of Cock Line Mersey tugs made fast to the massive structure, and with tow lines strained to breaking point, engines on maximum power, began the awesome task of getting this monster out of her building dock. Tug after tug joined in the struggle until in all ten were engaged. Thousands watched, but nothing appeared to be happening. Then slowly, almost imperceptibly, the colossus moved away from her berth. At this point the Cock Line brought into action their best tug, the immensely powerful *Black Cock*. After she had got her hawser fast and started towing, the dock made more rapid progress. The vast crowd now began to cheer, and with the flotilla of tugs sounding out on their sirens, the dock made her way out into the Mersey. Later it was the *Black Cock* and the *Storm Cock* that had the great responsibility of towing the dock from the Mersey to Portsmouth. She was 680 feet long and 144 feet wide. She was designed to service the heaviest of battleships, having a lifting capacity of 32,000 tons. In her starboard wall there was a fine range of workshops. These included a complete coppersmiths' shop. High above were located numerous heavy cranes, whilst firmly fixed in the walls were eight powerful steam-driven capstans, made by Hadfield & Company, for warping ships into position.

It was at this point in the history of the yard that Mr Restal R. Bevis was acting as managing director of the firm. Born in Rio de Janeiro, he was to spend almost all of his working life with Cammell Laird & Co., though he did serve for a time as a marine engineer with the National Steam Ship Company and the Pacific Steam Navigation Company. A member of the Institute of Civil Engineers and of the

H.M.S. Audacious, 1913.

Council of the Institute of Naval Architects, and therefore well suited for his very responsible position, Bevis was well-known as the patentee of many useful inventions connected with marine turbines and other machinery.

On May 30th 1912 there occurred an event of great importance at Laird's yard, namely the launching of the 5,400-ton cruiser *Melbourne*, which had been built for the Australian Commonwealth. This vessel was designed by Sir Phillip Watts, Chief Constructor of the Navy. She was 456 feet long, and protection was afforded along the whole of the ship with 2 inch thick armour plating. She carried eight 6 inch guns, and had two broadside torpedo tubes. The wireless telegraphy installation was described at the time as "being to the very latest Admiralty requirements". There were also four searchlights – placed in suitable positions – and a "comprehensive arrangement" of voice pipes, telegraphs, and telephones. The *Melbourne* carried a crew of 400 officers and men. The ship was propelled by steam turbines of the Parsons type. It is also interesting to note that all the steel forgings required for the turbines were manufactured at the Shipbuilders' Steel works at Sheffield.

More Admiralty orders were now being placed with the Birkenhead yard – for cruisers, destroyers, and the famous battleship, H.M.S. *Audacious* – later to be sunk in the First World War.

The bold reconstruction policy was now obviously starting to bear dividends. From the P & O Line came orders for two passenger–cargo liners, the *Khiva* and the *Khyber* – each of nearly 9,000 tons. From the newly formed Den Norske Line orders for two liners of 10,625 tons – the *Bergensfjord* and the *Kristianiafjord*. The *Bergensfjord* was launched on March 8th 1913. The vessel was 510 feet long and 61 feet broad, and designed to carry 105 first, 216 second and 700 third class passengers – the latter, untypical for the period, in remarkably good accommodation. She was, to an appreciable extent, an emigrant ship, for there was then a great traffic between Norway and America, with no less than 20,000 people emigrating each year. On this clientele the Line counted for their success. In fact the number of Norwegians in the United States in 1913 was astonishing; there were then over 1,000,000 born of Norwegian parents. To put this figure into perspective, the total population of Norway at this time was only 2,300,000!

After the launching ceremony Herr Cath Bang, for the Line, made the very valid point that it was a very big undertaking for a small country like Norway to start a new Atlantic service, particularly when the intensity of competition on this route was considered. It was, however, the great support shown to them, both at home and in America that had encouraged them to proceed. On the emigrant issue, he noted that many emigrants had already made a fortune in the New World, and were wishing

SS *Kristianiafjord*

Leonard

Boiler for Train Ferry Leonard

to return to their homeland. Under existing circumstances all such people had been obliged to take a passage in a foreign line, with all the inconvenience that that entailed. At last they would have a line of their own, and, he was glad to say, one with first-class ships, in which particular attention had been paid to the well-being of third class passengers, comparable accommodation for this class existing in no other line. In fact the accommodation for this class was good, being, untypically, located on the upper decks, where they were given accommodation in excellent two, four, six and eight berth cabins – a far cry from the early days in the Transatlantic Emigrant Trade!

Since 1908 there has been no member of the Laird family acting as Chairman of the Company. In that year J. MacGregor Laird relinquished this post. His place was taken by a Dr Francis Elgar, F.R.S., who had previously been the Managing Director of another shipbuilding company, Fairfield Shipbuilding & Engineering. His reign at Lairds, however, was but a brief one for he died two years later in 1910. His place was taken by a younger man, William Lionel Hitchins, a financial adviser to the Indian and South African Governments. The post of Managing Director was now filled by Mr J.G. Carter after the retirement in 1912 of Mr R.R. Bevis. War was now on the horizon, and it was under this new management that the company moved into the war-time period.

In their tens of thousands young men volunteered to fight in this bloody conflict, many of whom would never return from the battlefields of Europe. Two complete companies were recruited from the Laird shipyard for service in the R.N.V.R., and they took part in the abortive Antwerp expedition. Soon the Admiralty was pressing Lairds to produce submarines, but the firm had anticipated this demand, having already opened an experimental submarine department. Submarines E41 to E46 consequently left the yard in 1915 and 1916, each one of these submarines being substantial vessels 176 feet long. During 1916 the motor torpedo destroyer boats H.M.S. *Hoste, Seymour, Grenville, Parker* and *Sairmarez* also left the yard. Among the famous ships built for the Royal Navy during the war years was the cruiser *Chester*, one of several Laird-built ships which fought at Jutland. The war effort of the firm was a distinguished one.

It is interesting to note here that the Laird-built light cruiser, H.M.S. *Caroline*, launched at the beginning of the First World War, is in existence seventy-five years later. She is now serving as the headquarters of the Ulster Division of the Royal Naval Reserve, afloat and well in Belfast Harbour. In 1982 she was docked for inspection and servicing, when it was found that she was in such good condition that further inspection of the hull would not be needed for many years. Her commanding officer at this time was Lieutenant Commander Sampson who stated that she was a tribute to her builders, Messrs Laird & Company of Birkenhead.

One of the most unusual vessels ever built by Lairds, or any other shipbuilding firm for that matter, was the ice breaking train ferry *Leonard*, built for the National Transcontinental Railway of Canada. The story behind the building of this unique ship is interesting. Railway construction in Canada was at its zenith, with the mighty Intercolonial in fierce competition with the Transcontinental Company. Lines were being needlessly duplicated, and it was under this pressure that a 1,800-mile stretch of the Transcontinental line was being blasted through the vast Canadian wilderness. The key link in this line had to be a bridge over the mighty St. Lawrence river, but this was not yet built! So it was that an interim means of getting trains across the river had to be found, hence the Laird-built ferry *Leonard*.

Launched on January 17th 1914, she sailed for Canada on August 14th. Her principle dimensions were, length 326 feet, beam 65 feet, with a draft of just 15 feet. The trains were carried on what was described as a "tidal deck", on three lengths of track about 270 feet long. According to the state of the tides, this deck would be raised and lowered to link up with the lines, the gearing arrangements built into the ship by Lairds being capable of raising and lowering this deck, and a train and locomotive weighing about 1,400 tons at a rate of one foot per minute. The site of this ferry, later to be a bridge crossing, was at the mouth of the Chaudiere River, six miles upriver from Quebec City. The ice breaking capability of the ship was of course absolutely necessary, for ice can remain on the St Lawrence until May, blocking the river to all ordinary vessels. The whole venture was a bizarre one, but it did cause the production of a very remarkable vessel.

During the war years experimental work on engine design was continued. The end result of these labours was an opposed type engine suitable for application to merchant vessels, subsequently known as the Fullagar engine. The system was that ships would be propelled by diesel-electric machinery, the dynamos being driven by a set of Fullagar engines, which could develop about 3,000 horse-power. The first ship to be fitted out with this new system was the vessel named after the system, the 150 feet long Anchor Brocklebank coaster *Fullagar*.

Train Ferry, Leonard.

Ark Royal

Handed over to the owners on July 22nd 1920, she was far from being a handsome vessel to look at, being, as Masefield put it, nothing but a "Dirty British coaster with a salt-caked smoke stack". After one year the Brocklebank Line sold her to the Isle of Man Steam Packet Company, who changed her name to *Caria*, and traded her to the island from Liverpool for the next five years. In 1926 she was sold again to the British Columbia Cement Company Ltd. of Vancouver, and, once more she was re-christened, this time as the *Shean*. On October 24th 1930, she was going at full speed off Victoria, B.C., when suddenly there was a tremendous crash, followed by the shattering sound of tearing metal. The unlucky coaster had hit a submerged rock! At the time of this mishap she was carrying 10,000 bags of cement. Amazingly she did not sink, but made port and was soon repaired. She really owed her survival to one fact, that she was a 'welded' ship, not one that had been merely riveted – the normal practice at this time. The case for the all-welded ship was made abundantly clear by this one accident.

After being laid up during the world-wide depression she was sold once more, this time to Senor O. Rodriguez, who once again changed her name, the *Fullagar* now sailing as the *Cedros*. Registered at Ensenada in Lower Califonia she spent the first part of the 1930s trading in this area, but exactly what missions she carried out for Senor Rodriguez remain something of a mystery. The end of this Laird-built coaster was a sad one, for on August 31st 1937 she put out from Ensenada bound for Nazatlan in Mexico. Thirty miles south east of her home port she collided with the M.V. *Hildalgo*. The *Hildalgo* managed to make port but the *Fullagar* (or *Cedros*) quietly sank below the calm blue waters of the Pacific Ocean.

Other notable orders dealt with by the firm in the 1920s included three 5,360-ton fruit-carrying steamers, built to the order of Messrs Elders & Fyffes and the French Government Mail Steamer *Gouverneur General Chanzy*, which latter vessel is certainly worthy of a passing mention. Launched in May 1921, she had been built to the order of Le Commission aux Transport Maritime et a la Marine Merchande, for mail, passenger and cargo service on the run from Marseilles to Algiers. A two-decked vessel, she had been built to a very high standard under special survey of the Bureau Veritas to class + (1) 3/3 M.11, and to comply with the French Government regulations.

Accommodation on this ship was for 162 first class passengers, and fifty-six third class passengers, in addition to officers and crew. Interestingly arrangements had also been made in the lower 'tween

Gouverneur General Chanzy

decks for the transportation of troops, and horse stalls were fitted at the fore end of the upper deck. Mechanical ventilation was installed throughout the ship, which included the holds in view of the fact that fruit formed the chief cargo. The propelling machinery consisted of two sets of Parsons' turbines, designed to give an average speed of 19 knots. Although the boilers were intended to burn fuel oil, they were designed so that they could readily be converted for coal burning.

The 19,848-ton passenger liner *Samaria* was also launched by the firm in the spring of 1922. She was the latest addition to the already imposing fleet of the Cunard Company, and was designed for the Line's service from Liverpool to Boston and New York. She was the largest liner built on Mersey-side to burn fuel oil. The *Samaria* was a sister ship to the *Scythia*, and was a typical unit of the Cunard Company's post First World War fleet, having a single funnel, oil-fired, and driven by double-reduction geared turbines. The service speed of the vessel was 16 knots.

As one might expect on a Cunard Line vessel the accommodation on the *Samaria* was exceptionally good. The total number of passengers she could carry was 2,180, of which 336 were first class, 340 second class, and the remaining 1,504 third class. Typical of transatlantic liners of this period there was ample promenading space, both open and covered for all classes. A special feature of this facility for first class passengers was the "Garden Lounge", but the second class passengers had a splendid verandah cafe for their exclusive use. The first class public rooms were all arranged with entrances leading from the main staircase, which formed a handsome central hall; an oval lounge, decorated in Chinese style, was a particular feature of this part of the ship.

On the outbreak of war in 1939, the *Samaria*, with other Cunard Line ships was requisitioned as a transport and subsequently steamed 280,000 miles on war service, carrying 179,000 passengers. In June 1953 she was one of the ships assembled at Spithead for the Coronation Royal Naval Review. She was finally broken up in 1956.

The next launch of significance from the yard was also that of a transatlantic liner, the 17,000-ton passenger and cargo screw-steamer *De Grasse*, built to the order of the Compagnie Generale Trans-atlantique, of Havre and Paris, for their New York service. Launched on February 23rd 1924, she was handed over to her owners in August. A special feature of the *De Grasse* was the decoration, which was designed and carried out by three well-known French firms, whose workers had been sent

De Grasse

Ballroom, Mauretania

Interior view of Mauretania.

H.M.S. Rodney

over to Birkenhead for that purpose. The passenger accommodation extended over six decks. The state rooms of the first class had wood cot beds throughout, and somewhat ahead of the time, many had private bathrooms.

The propelling machinery consisted of two sets of Parsons turbines driving twin screws through single reduction mechanical gearing, designed to give a large ratio of reduction. After the trials, which took place in August, command of the new 17-knot liner was given to Captain Roberts, who, with his large crew, took her back to France for her maiden voyage on August 21st.

Order No. 904 was for H.M.S. *Rodney*, which, at 35,000 tons, was designed to be the largest and most powerful warship the world had ever seen. *Rodney's* keel was laid in December 1922, her launch being three years later in December 1925. The day of her launch was a great one in the history of Cammell Laird & Company, for the Princess Mary had been given the honour of naming the vessel.

On the morning of December 17th, 15,000 people made their way to the Yard to watch the great event. At 10.30 am the yard buzzer blew, the signal for every employee in the yard and office to cease work, their number soon swelling the crowd until it was 20,000 strong. On the platform, erected before the bows of the huge battleship, 2,000 prominent Merseyside citizens were gathered. A short service then took place, followed by an equally short shower of rain. Meanwhile, far below, men were working hard to remove the shores and blocks which kept the battleship a prisoner.

The Managing Director of Cammell Laird's, Mr R.S. Johnson, then placed in the Princess's hands the usual bottle of wine, which was attached to a notably patriotic cord made of red, white and blue silk. No doubt due to lack of experience in hurling bottles, Her Royal Highness threw the bottle at *Rodney's* bows, but alas, without enough force. Much to the embarrassment of all concerned it then swung, still intact, far out of reach. After much frantic activity, and no doubt a few nervous break-downs, the bottle was eventually hauled in and handed to the Princess. She tried again, but this time achieved what would seem to be the impossible, failing to hit the 35,000-ton bulk of the great battle-ship just a few feet in front of her completely! Being Merseyside, one of Laird's workers then came to the rescue, yelling out – "Third time does it". Morale suitably boosted, she tried once more – this time, thankfully, scoring a direct hit – and broke the bottle.

Slowly H.M.S. *Rodney* began to move, and to the cheers of the 20,000 present, very gracefully slid into the river. The launch had of necessity been timed for an exceptionally high tide, so many small vessels were riding at anchor, high up, and clearly visible to the thousands of spectators. They pro-vided a curious back-drop to the launching of this great twentieth century ship. On one side a small fleet of fishing smacks were riding at anchor. Nearer to was a great wind-jammer, with the old wooden-wall training ship *Conway* some distance away in the far background. By chance these were the only vessels visible to the dignitaries high on the ceremonial platform, inadvertently providing a scene that could have existed over a hundred years ago.

The scene soon changed though as a flotilla of tugs raced towards *Rodney*, anxious to get lines on board to secure the mighty man-o-war. She slowly turned to face upstream, looking at this point not the least bit like a battleship. Much of her armour still had to be added, which would then make her ride lower in the water, giving her the well-known low profile of one of these ships. After a while she came alongside the ancient *Conway*. The latter had been considered a large ship in her day, but side by side with *Rodney* she now seemed a mere fishing smack.

Almost two years later work on the *Rodney* was completed. In all she had cost the nation over £7,000,000, and had been under construction in Laird's yard for nearly five years. She had a length of 702 feet and a breadth of 100 feet. This great warship had three forward turrets, each of which contained three 16 inch guns. She also had a number of smaller weapons. *Rodney* packed a deadly broadside for her day, for her big guns could hurl a projectile of 2,340 pounds twenty miles, and at each full broadside the ship was capable of hurling into space almost ten tons of shell.

The ship was manned by a crew of 1,200 officers and men when she was put in commission. In August 1927, with a smaller crew on board she was prepared for her passage round the coast to Portsmouth. On Saturday, August 13th, excited crowds on the ferry boats, and on both banks of the Mersey, waited to watch the departure of the great ship. At 11.00 am she was still in her dock at Birkenhead, but just forty-five minutes later she was out in the stream, and almost free of the attendant tugs and ready for her first trip under her own power.

Thousands of people watched as she made her stately progress down the river, who, thanks to the splendid sunshine, were afforded a superb view of the mighty ship. *Rodney* had a bomb-proof deck of hardened steel, and was protected by exceptionally thick armour against attack from the air. She was also designed to resist the simultaneous explosion of four torpedoes under the water-line. During the Second World War, which she survived, she took part in the sinking of the German battleship *Bismark*, played a notable role in the 'D' Day landings, and protected many convoys. She was finally broken up in 1948.

It was during the 1920s that Messrs Laird & Company built some notable vessels for the famous Blue Star Line. Order No. 919 was for the *Almeda*, order No. 920 for the *Andalucia*, order No. 921 for the *Arandora*, all of them vessels of some 13,000 tons, specially designed for the Line's passenger and meat service to South America, to run a fortnightly service between London and the capitals of Brazil and Argentina. The head of the Blue Star Line at this time was Lord Vestey. The growth of the line had been phenomenal. In 1914 their fleet had been composed of six steamers of a total of 30,000 tons gross. Two years later the fleet had doubled to twelve steamers of 63,000 tons gross. In 1925, not allowing for the above vessels then under construction at Birkenhead, they had eighteen vessels of 111,000 tons gross, and with the nine new steamers then planned or under construction, they were heading to the point when they would have twenty-seven vessels of over 200,000 tons gross. The Vestey and Blue Star venture was based on the meat and passenger trade between the United Kingdom, and Argentina, the aforementioned Laird built ships being intended at the time to allow for the running of a fortnightly service between London and the capitals of Brazil and Argentina.

The *Almeda*, typical of all three of these ships, was launched at Birkenhead on Tuesday, June 26th 1926. The passenger accommodation on the ship extended over the four upper decks, while all the 'tween decks below the upper deck and also the holds were insulated for the meat cargoes. The accommodation on this ship was what was described as 'first-class de luxe service' only, which was provided for about 180 passengers. Special features of the accommodation were the number of state rooms with *en suite* facilities. A gymnasium was fitted out on the lower promenade deck, and other large open spaces were provided for promenading, games etc. The crew's quarters were located on the upper deck, and fitted out in a manner which was described as 'comfortable' but it should perhaps be noticed, by way of contrast to those sleeping in the 'first-class de luxe' section of the ship, that their rooms were fitted with galvanised iron berths!

For the remainder of the 1920s the yard remained busy with a variety of orders which included the Latex Carriers *Greystoke Castle* and *Munster Castle*, both vessels of just under 6,000 tons, built for J. Chambers & Company. Order No.930, which was shipped on April 30th 1928, was for the tin dredger *Kamunting*, an electrically-operated vessel some 150 feet long, built to the order of the Kamunting Tin Dredging Company. During the year of 1928 the yard produced an entire fleet of ships for the

Canadian National West Indies Steamship Company, these being the *Lady Nelson, Lady Drake, Lady Hawkins, Lady Rodney,* and *Lady Somers,* all of them very substantial passenger and cargo vessels of about 9,000 tons.

The 966th vessel launched by the yard was also for a Canadian organisation, the 6,893-ton *Prince Henry,* a passenger and cargo ship built to the order of the Canadian National Steamship Company Limited. The launch of this ship took place on January 17th 1930, the ceremony being performed by Ishbel MacDonald, the Prime Minister's daughter. This ship was one of three similar vessels launched at Birkenhead in 1930 for Canadian National, the other two being the *Prince David* and the *Prince Robert.* The total value of these orders was in the region of £2,500,000.

These three ships had been built for Canadian National's Pacific Coast-Alaskan service, which they operated between the ports of Vancouver, Seattle, Victoria, Prince Rupert and the Alaskan ports of Ketchikan, Wrangell, Juneau and Skagway, the gateway to Dawson, the Yukon and the Klondike of Gold Rush fame. Trade in these waters was in fact booming at this time with machinery and supplies going out and the products of this wild, untamed land flowing back – timber, minerals, fish etc. There had also just been a tremendous growth of interest in this area as a holiday playground with people coming up in their thousands from the Pacific and Western States to visit British Columbia, a trend which, as we know today, has continued.

An interesting event took place at Cammell Laird's shipyard on May 29th 1930, when two 484-ton Mersey Ferry Boats were launched from the same slipway, one lined up behind the other! The vessels were the *Thurstaston* and the *Claughton,* both twin-screw vessels capable of crossing the Mersey at 12 knots. Constructed of mild steel, both were 158 feet long by 40 feet wide. The seating capacity of each of these boats was 162, but each one had a Board of Trade Certificate to carry 1,400 passengers and a crew of nine. The construction of the vessels had been carried out under the supervision of Captain Langshaw, the Manager of the Ferries.

Mrs McVey, wife of Alderman C. McVey, and Mrs Newman, wife of Mr E. A. Newman, deputy chairman of the Ferries Committee, were the two ladies honoured by being asked to launch the boats. Mr R.S. Johnson presided at the lunch that followed. In his speech afterwards he pointed out that his firm had very ancient connections with the Mersey Ferry Service, for in the 1840's they had built the already-mentioned ferry *Nun.* He was not sure what had happened since that time, for, until an order was obtained from the Corporation in 1925, they never had another order! In 1925 though the Corporation suddenly realised there was a shipbuilding firm in Birkenhead, and actually placed an order. In his obviously tongue-in-cheek speech he said he would not want anyone present to run away with the idea that the Ferries Committee had been very generous to Cammell Laird's, one of the methods used to get the price down being a veiled threat to take the order to the Clyde! All of which caused much laughter from the council officers present.

In his reply Alderman McVey struck a more serious note by drawing attention to the now growing problem of unemployment in Birkenhead, and appealing to shipowners to place orders with the excellent local firm of Cammell Laird's for their ships. He continued by pointing out that during the war period the yard had employed about 14,000 workers, but in 1930 that was down to (only!) 7,000. He continued in optimist style, by stating that he frankly and honestly hoped that the firm was not going to build any more warships, as he thought the time had arrived when these vessels would go out of existence altogether. He concluded by wishing the firm well in its rationalisation plans as this would make it a better prospect for socialisation in the future, but on the other hand wished the firm success as it was, as this would mean men would be working in the yard rather than walking the streets unemployed.

Alas though the post-war depression was hitting the big armament firms badly, forcing firms such as Vickers Armstrong, Beardmore, John Brown, and others to take drastic measures to save their respective firms. Laird's was the last of these big enterprises to face up to the problem, which, in March 1932, involved the writing-off of £3,500,000 capital. In his speech at the sixty-eighth annual meeting of the company, the Chairman acknowledged that the limitation of armaments might be a good thing, for this country and the world, but it seemed sad that it had to be carried out at the expense of one section of the community, particularly when that section had played a significant part in the recent war. In Germany though matters were even worse, for unemployment had now reached 5 million, Adolph Hitler and his fascist thugs were on the march, and within twelve months he was being voted into power. In 1935 Germany announced the re-introduction of compulsory military service – sadly war, not peace, was once more on the agenda for humanity, and in the forthcoming struggles Laird-built ships were, as before, to play a significant role.

Unemployment, hardship and suffering continued to plague the shipyard workers of Birkenhead throughout the early 1930s, when many men considered themselves to be lucky if they obtained one day's work each week. Work at the Yard did continue though, albeit on a reduced scale, but on October 10th 1934 there was, once again, a significant launch at Laird's yard. The significance of this launch was that it was the thousandth launch to be conducted at the yard. The vessel concerned being the first of two vessels being built at the Yard for the Booth Steamship Company, the 5,000-ton cargo vessel *Clement*. Her sister ship the *Crispin* was to follow her into the water less than a month later on December 12th. Perhaps because of the unemployment, this launch was watched by the largest number of sightseers since H.M.S. *Rodney* was put into the water. Soon though the fortunes of the yard began to turn, for Laird's were shortly to obtain orders for two vessels that were to mark a milestone in the history of shipbuilding on the Mersey. One of these orders was to come from the Cunard Company headquarters, just across the Mersey in Liverpool, the other from the Admiralty.

On March 13th 1935, the local press announced that Cammell Laird's was to build an aircraft carrier, which order would result in three year's work for 2,000 men. The Admiralty announcement, made the previous day, informed the public that the vessel would have a displacement of 10,000 tons, that she would cost between £2 million and £2.5 million, be the largest ship to be built on Merseyside and that she would be named the *Ark Royal*! Councillor Baker, Mayor of Birkenhead, responded to this news by saying that it was very gratifying, especially as there were something like 8,000 unemployed shipyard workers on Merseyside, the greater proportion of whom were in Birkenhead. Work on this great ship was soon in hand, but before she was launched the keelplates of an even greater man-o'-war were to be laid, this for the 10th battleship to be built by the Company.

On January 1st 1937 between 4,000 and 5,000 people looked down from specially-constructed platforms in Laird's yard to watch the ceremony of laying the first keelplates of the *Prince of Wales* which was to be one of the most powerful battleships in the world. The cost of this 35,000-ton ship was to be £7 million, with an estimated £5.5 million of this sum being spent directly on local wages. The scene at this ceremony was an impressive one, for the keel of H.M.S. *Prince of Wales* was to be laid alongside the slipway now occupied by the almost completed aircraft carrier *Ark Royal*. These were indeed exciting days at Laird's shipyard, for the berth to be vacated by the carrier would soon be occupied by the new Cunard White Star Line passenger ship, the order for which had at last been finally confirmed just a few days previously.

H.M.S. Ark Royal 1937

The thunder of the salute from nineteen guns awoke the whole of Merseyside at 8.00 am on the morning of April 13th 1937. *Ark Royal*, pride of Birkenhead's craftsmanship and skill was about to be launched. 30,000 people soon began making their way to the Yard to watch the great event. This was the greatest crowd that had ever witnessed a launch in Great Britain. Not since the launch of H.M.S. *Rodney*, a dozen years previously had a shipyard ceremony created such a stir. The whole of Merseyside had, it seemed suspended its usual activity for this historic event. The ferry boats were crowded with passengers anxious to get a good view of the launch, whilst three to four thousand people thronged Liverpool Pier Head, and on the Birkenhead side the crowds were even greater. There were people silhouetted against the clear blue sky on the huge roof of the Great Western Railway sheds, and others looked down from the Birkenhead Town Hall clock tower.

The lady given the honour of launching H.M.S. *Ark Royal* was Lady Maude Hoare, D.B.E., wife of the First Lord of the Admiralty. High on the platform above the vast crowd Mr Johnson, head of the firm, handed Lady Maude a bottle of Empire wine, very tastefully decorated with red, white and blue ribbons – and lucky white heather. After a short speech concluding with: "I name this ship *Ark Royal*. May God guide her and guard and keep all who sail in her", she gripped the bottle firmly and heaved it with all her might at the side of the ship. Alas, history was about to repeat itself, for although Laird's could build fine ships they clearly had problems selecting bottles of wine that would break on impact with the bows of a ship! Without loss of dignity, Lady Maude tried again, this time putting as much force behind the throw as was humanly possible. Her effort was rewarded by a dull thud. She tried once more, but still nothing happened, when above the silence rose a solitary voice from a local wit, with the familiar local dictum: "Give it to Dixie!" On the fourth attempt the bottle smashed into atoms.

The brooding mass of H.M.S. *Ark Royal* remained stationary for what seemed ages, but in reality was but a few moments. Mr Johnson and his executives watched with unconcealed anxiety, hoping and praying that she would start to move. Tension mounted as the huge crowd watched and waited in complete silence, when at last an excited voice rang out: "She's moving! She's moving!" and a full-throated roar rang out, so loud that it could be heard on the far banks of the Mersey. Schoolboys watched with awe, whilst old hands in the Yard looked on with pride as *Ark Royal* carried its thousands of tons down the well-greased slipway. The band played "Rule Britannia" whilst the crowd continued to cheer, as the great ship came to life.

Out in the river a dozen tugs speeded to her assistance, ready to tow her round to the wet basin. Her anchor was dropped with a rattle that could be heard far down the river – as the eyes of thousands viewed with wonder this masterpiece of engineering and naval architecture; yet another triumphant achievement of Cammell Laird & Company. The *Ark Royal* was the third ship of her name in naval annals. She had a displacement of 22,000 tons, was 800 feet long and had a maximum beam of ninety-five feet. Her huge engines generated 102,000 horse-power for which she carried 4,620 tons of fuel oil. Her complement was 1,575 officers and men. Her first commander was Captain, later Rear Admiral A.J. Power, C.B., C.V.O. In all she carried sixty aircraft; five squadrons composed of Blackburn Skuas and Fairey Swordfish – primitive flying machines by the standards of today, for the two-seater Skuas only had a top speed of 200 miles per hour, but could, nevertheless carry a 500 pound bomb load.

During the uneasy summer of 1939 the politicians of the Western Democracies did all that was possible to avert war, whilst at the same time the Royal Navy was carefully making plans, based on the, by now, more realistic assumption that war would break out. On August 31st H.M.S. *Ark Royal* put to sea, her mission being to join the Home Fleet on patrol in the waters between Shetland and Norway. The following day, September 1st, Germany invaded Poland. Hitler's armies were on the march and soon all of Europe would be aflame. On September 3rd, when *Ark Royal* was taking up her station, in the cold wastes of the North Sea, Britain and France declared war on Germany. This devastating news was soon relayed to H.M. Home Fleet, exactly one hour later *Ark Royal's* bosun's mate going to the microphone below the bridge and shouting "D'ye hear there?", the preliminary call for all announcements. Captain Powers followed him: "This is the Captain speaking", he said. "I have just received the signal: 'Commence hostilities against Germany'."

Hostilities began in earnest for *Ark Royal* on September 14th when she was on a submarine hunt with four destroyers and was suddenly attacked. This was to be but the first of many wartime battles that the *Ark* was to be engaged in. One of her most notable missions was to join with other British warships in the historic hunt for the giant German battleship *Admiral Graf Spee*. It was after a long hunt that the *Graf Spee* was finally engaged by H.M.S. *Ajax*, *Exeter* and *Achilles*, whilst off the River

Plate and sought refuge in Montevideo. Force K which then included the *Ark* was ordered to refuel at Rio, and then proceed to the Plate. On December 17th, *Ark Royal* put into Rio, refuelled and set sail again once more, bound for the River Plate, her mighty engines driving her through the tropical waters at 25 knots. Shortly after midnight, though, a signal reached the *Ark* informing all on board that the German Commander had scuttled his ship outside Montevideo harbour rather than fight. The long hunt was over but the *Ark's* aircraft had been baulked of their prey.

On June 18th 1940, the *Ark Royal* sailed from Scapa to join Force H at Gibraltar. Soon the Italians were joining with their German allies in making false claims about the *Ark* being hit or sunk. It was the *Ark* though that was doing the hitting, with raids upon Oran in North Africa, Cagliari in Sardinia and Genoa, Spezia, Pisa and Leghorn in Italy, all mounted from the great Birkenhead-built carrier. Except for short spells of duty elsewhere, the *Ark* served for eighteen successful months on convoy duty and mounting airborne raids in the Western basin of the Mediterranean.

After being involved in the historic battle which ended with the sinking of the *Bismark* the *Ark* returned to Gibraltar where she once more resumed her operations with Force H in the Mediterranean. On November 13th 1941, she was heading towards Gibraltar when there was a large explosion under the bridge. The *Ark* had been hit by a torpedo. Serious damage was done, but only one member of the crew, Able Seaman E. Mitchell, had been killed. Soon the great ship had a list of twelve degrees. By 4.00 pm, the *Ark Royal* had heeled over to an angle of eighteen degrees, and the list was increasing. The destroyer *Legion* was brought alongside, and in a short time 1,540 officers and men were transferred to this smaller vessel.

The few men now left on board *Ark Royal* worked like trojans to save her, setting up pumps, but soon all power failed, and conditions became steadily worse. The destroyer *Laforey* was brought alongside to provide power, and steam was raised once more, but they were fighting a losing battle. At 2.15 on the morning of the 14th a fire broke out in the port boiler-room, all salvage work came to a halt, as the list now increased to twenty degrees. With the ship apparently about to capsize, men were ordered into the tug *St. Day*. At 0430 Captain Maund slid down into the tug to be greeted with a cheer. At 0600 the flight deck of H.M.S. *Ark Royal* was vertical and the island lying flat upon the sea. The men on the screening destroyers watched and waited for the inevitable to happen. Thirteen minutes later the end came. "She's gone," said one of the watchers, and it was some time before anyone could speak.

Quietly, and with great dignity, H.M.S. *Ark Royal* slid below the surface of the Mediterranean on her last journey down 1,000 fathoms. And it is here that she lies today, just a few short miles from Gibraltar. Ships may need no tombstones for their names live on, particularly that of H.M.S. *Ark Royal III*, which fought so valiantly in a very noble cause, but what a wonderful thing it would be if she could be raised and brought back to Birkenhead, as a tribute to those who served in her, and to the highly-skilled men of Merseyside who built her.

H.M.S. Chester, a 430ft long cruiser launched on 15th May 1916.

Chapter 4

1937-1991

The keel of the Cunard White Star liner *Mauretania* had been laid on No. 6 slipway in May 1937, the previous occupant of this berth being H.M.S. *Ark Royal*. Soon 5,000 men were employed on the job of building this great ship, each one lavishing care and attention on every detail. When completed she was to be the largest ship ever built in an English shipyard. Almost unbelievably, just over one year later, the *Mauretania* was due to be launched! Thirty thousand people had turned out to witness the launch of the *Ark Royal*, but this figure was nothing to compare to the numbers who were soon to watch the launch of the Cunard Line's latest liner at Birkenhead.

Without a doubt July 24th 1938 was the greatest day in the history of Cammell Laird's and Birkenhead – the day when the *Mauretania* was launched. No-one will really know for sure just how many people watched this launch, for estimates vary from 50,000 to 300,000, but an indication of the numbers can be obtained from these facts. For miles along the Rock Ferry coast thousands stood for hours waiting for the great moment, whilst Tranmere beach was just a solid mass of spectators. The yard itself was filled to capacity, but on the Liverpool side of the river the scene was incredible. Here spectators stood in an almost unbroken line for over six miles! Even the roof of Liverpool's new Cathedral was jammed full with people. On the murky waters of the Mersey itself there were ferry boats, launches, barges and even rowing boats all crammed with sightseers.

When Lady Bates, wife of the Chairman of the Cunard White Star Line, unveiled the nameplate of the vessel and crashed the bottle of champagne against her bows the river became a tumult. Sirens screamed, maroons were fired whilst tens of thousands cheered and cheered. Overhead planes roared and on the river itself scores of ships' sirens added to the clamour. It took just 45 seconds for the 17,660-ton shell of the *Mauretania* to glide 780 feet down the slipway and into the Mersey. She swept half-a-mile out into the river before her anchor was let go and eight attendant tugs took control of her. She was, without a doubt a magnificent ship, her accommodation for passengers being up to the usual high standards set by Cunard.

Exceptional luxury and spacious layouts characterised the passenger space in all classes. There were in all over twenty public rooms, in addition to which was an observation lounge and cocktail bar facing forward. On the same deck there was a magnificently decorated 'Grand Hall' fitted with a dance floor, a shopping centre, lounge, smoke room, writing room, cinema, child-

Mauretania under construction.

Mauretania at launching.

Mauretania at launching.

Mauretania, ship no. 1029.

Mauretania: arrival in London.

Mauretania: arrival in London.

ren's room and library. The third-class accommodation was on a scale never before attempted in an Atlantic liner of her time, for there was an unusually large number of two-berth rooms, both tourist and third-class also having their own cinemas. In addition to all of this the 'Keep fit' enthusiasts were well catered for with two gymnasiums, a swimming pool and a Turkish bath.

Mauretania II had a reputation to live up to, for her predecessor had been the holder of the coveted North Atlantic "Blue Riband" for twenty-two years for having made the fastest crossing of the Western Ocean. Laird's *Mauretania* was a couple of thousand tons bigger than the first Cunarder to bear this famous name, but at 22 knots she was fully 10 knots slower than the older clipper-built vessel. After being fitted out and undergoing the usual trials the 'Mauretania' was ready to make her maiden voyage across the Atlantic to New York. She sailed from the Mersey on this passage at 7.15 pm on June 17th 1939 to the cheers of thousands of spectators and the blasts of sirens from ships moored in the river, which included the famous *Riena del Pacifico*.

Just six days and nineteen hours later *Mauretania II* arrived in New York City. As she sailed proudly up the Hudson River she signalled her arrival by great booms on her siren, the sound of which could travel for up to eleven miles. Tens of thousands watched from the waterfront, cheering and waving in the bright sunshine, as aircraft circled her and the New York Fireboats put on their special water-cascade display, reserved for such great occasions. The tumult increased as scores of other vessels in port all responded to the Cunarder by sounding their sirens.

Her send off at Liverpool had been tremendous, as was her welcome at New York, but neither was to compare with the welcome tribute still in store for her. Leaving New York she then set sail for London, where she arrived on August 6th. She was the largest ship ever to sail up the Thames, and as she made her way up the river to her new berth, the King George V Dock, an estimated 100,000 spectators lined the banks from Tilbury onwards, all cheering, shouting and waving their greetings to the *Mauretania*, this most spectacular creation of the Laird shipyard, Birkenhead.

Alas though, *Mauretania* was not to sail for long as a civilian liner for just four weeks after Hitler had declared war she was singled out for particular attention by the German forces, After making only four voyages she was assigned to troop carrying work. The close of 1939 found her in New York once more, but not as a luxury liner. Now stripped of the most luxurious furniture and fittings ever put into a ship she rapidly prepared for wartime service.

The *Mauretania* sailed from New York early in 1940. A United States military guard was put on board when she passed through the Panama Canal in March of that year. There she attracted a good deal of attention that must have seriously embarrassed those responsible for the safety of the great liner. The Italians showed a great interest in the movement of the ship which was to play such a notable role in their impending defeat. Gleefully they informed the world that she was steaming on a course which would take her past the northern coast of the Galapagos Islands, where there was a heavy concentration of German U-boats, who would no doubt soon finish her off!

The Italians (and the Germans) were to be disappointed though, for on April 5th, the *Mauretania* arrived safely at Honolulu. She was blacked out and stopped only to refuel. It was after she left Honolulu that she began her secret wartime career. A security black-out was, in a sense, even more necessary for her than for the famous "Queens". Their greatest protection throughout their wartime service was their great turn of speed, something which the *Mauretania* lacked, for although a fast ship she was still seven to eight knots slower than the express Cunarders. A list of the *Mauretania's* war-time ports of call show that hardly a name is missing, yet throughout this crucial period she moved like a phantom over the oceans of the globe – rumour and report never catching up with her. During the war years she sailed over half-a-million miles and carried some 335,000 fighting men to all parts of the world.

September 1946 found the *Mauretania* safely back in Gladstone Dock, Liverpool, with the first of over 1,000 Laird's workers descending on her to begin the giant task of reconverting the 35,000-ton liner from her seven years of troop carrying back to the comfort and luxury of a great peace-time Cunarder. Soon the number of workers was increased to a daily average of 1,500 so that by December 11th work was well in hand and attention was given to removing the seventy-six-ton after funnel.

The newly-fitted *Mauretania* was soon back at work again, on the run from the United Kingdom to the United States of America, but sadly, under a major Cunard re-organisation plan, she sailed from Southampton, not Liverpool. From now on her visits to the Mersey were to be few and far between. For the better part of two decades the *Mauretania* continued to give excellent service to her owners, until, in November 1965, she made her last crossing from America back to Southampton. The greatest ship ever built by Cammell Laird and Company was about to be scrapped.

To mark this sad occasion messages were exchanged between the owners, Cunard, Mr Robert Johnson, Chairman of Lairds, and Captain J. Treasur Jones, who commanded the ship on her final Atlantic crossing, Captain Jones' message to Mr Johnson being:

> "I and my ship's company thank you for your greetings and good wishes on our final homecoming. This fine ship has been a credit to the Cunard Line, and to you as the builders. The *Mauretania* has always been a happy ship, and it is with a feeling of sadness we bring her home on her final voyage. We wish your fine company continued success."

Mauretania's final voyage was some ten days after her last Atlantic crossing when a skeleton crew took her to Inverkeithing in Fife to be broken up. She had been sold to Thomas W. Ward and Company of Sheffield for a figure which it is believed was in the region of £1,000,000.

During the Second World War Cammell Laird built 106 fighting ships – an average of one every twenty days, and thirteen other vessels. These included many submarines and the destroyers *Ulysses* and *Undaunted*. The company's repair department worked at an incredible pace throughout the war years, putting back into working order no less than 2,000 merchant vessels, nine battleships, eleven aircraft carriers and 100 other warships. For its work on two the battleship *Barham* and the aircraft carrier *Illustrious* Cammell Laird received commendation from the British Admiralty.

The Laird-built battleship *Prince of Wales* (35,000 tons) was completed for the Royal Navy and, within six weeks of delivery, she took part in the action which eventually destroyed the German battleship *Bismark*. Later *Prince of Wales* achieved distinction of a different kind, for it was aboard her in mid-Atlantic that Winston Churchill and Roosevelt signed the Atlantic Charter.

The war over, business at Cammell Laird's continued to be brisk, for the gaps in many merchant shipowner's fleets had to be filled, for losses had been heavy. Vessels that had served as troop carriers had to be converted back to civilian use. In addition to all this many merchant ships were now getting old and beyond economic repair, for there had been a six-year gap in merchant ship production. Petrol tankers were much in demand now and Laird's were foremost in meeting this need. For the famous Shaw Saville Line the Company built two very fine passenger and cargo liners, the *Corinthic* and the *Ceramic* and the general cargo vessel *Persic*. They were designed to operate on the run to Australia.

So far as ships for local service is concerned the company built a very handsome quintet of cross-channel steamers for the Isle of Man Steam Packet Company, and two for the Great Western Rail-

The 7117 Highland Laddie, launched on the 30th October 1909. A passenger and chilled meat vessel built for the Nelson Steam Navigation Co.

The 7365 ton Highland Brae, another passenger and chilled meat vessel, built for Nelson & Co, launched on 6th August 1910.

The 522 ton paddle steamer Kwang Tung, built for the Chinese Navy and launched on 4th March 1863.

Ark Royal

way, the *St. Patrick* and the *St. David*. Vessels soon began to run down the slipways for the Blue Funnel Line, the Booth Steamship Company, and the British and Continental Steamship Company.

It was now ten years since the craftsmen of Cammell Laird's had fashioned the hull of Britain's innovative aircraft carrier, the *Ark Royal*, when, in January 1946, it was announced that a successor to this famous ship was to be built at the Merseyside yard. Work on this new vessel – the fourth *Ark Royal* in the history of the Royal Navy – had been going on for some time, the fact of which was therefore public knowledge already, but given the British obsession with attempting to keep all things 'secret' it was only just being taken off Laird's 'secret' list!

She was to be built on the same stocks as her predecessor, and while her overall length was not to be so great, her displacement was to be greater. Few details were being made public at this time, apart from the fact that she was planned to carry 100 aircraft whereas the previous carrier of the same name had only carried eighty, and that all 'new devices' developed during the war would obviously be embodied in her. The cost of the new *Ark Royal* it was estimated at this point in time, was likely to exceed the £3,000,000 mark.

Writing at the time our local reporter on the *Birkenhead News* made the point that her construction would keep hundreds of men busy for the next twelve months, it not being considered that she would be ready for launching until late in 1947! Further to which, he continued, another two years work would be necessary to fit her out and make her ready to take her place among Britain's fighting ships. The news of all this, he concluded, should help to silence the rumours, then rife in the town, that Laird's were about to dismiss many workers. The *Ark Royal IV*, however, made a much greater contribution than this to keeping down local unemployment, for as it transpired it was fully a decade later before she was handed over complete, and ready for sea!

She was finally launched by Her Majesty Queen Elizabeth II in 1955, the first occasion on which a ship built on Merseyside had been launched by a Queen of England. Among *Ark Royal's* many features was an angled flight deck, which was to become a standard part of aircraft carrier design, a steam-operated catapult for launching aircraft, and sidelifts. Her engines were designed to generate 152,000 horse-power.

Ark Royal

Another notable warship built by Laird's was H.M.S. *Devonshire*, which was laid down in March 1959. She was the eighth ship to be called *Devonshire*, the name having been in constant use by the Royal Navy since 1692. She was to be Britain's first guided missile destroyer. 520 feet long she had a beam of 54 feet and a standard displacement of just over 5,000 tons. Her armaments consisted of one "Seaslug" guided weapons system mounted on the quarterdeck; four radar-controlled 4.5 inch guns in twin mountings forward, also two "Seacat" close range guided weapons systems fitted abaft the after funnel. For anti-submarine work she was fitted with the latest underwater detection equipment and she carried a Westland Wessex helicopter – the first to be fitted as a complete "hunter killer".

As was so often the case with Laird-built ships, H.M.S. *Devonshire* broke new ground in ship construction once more. She was fitted with an entirely new type of machinery. This consisted of two sets of geared steam turbines, for normal steaming conditions, with gas turbines to provide additional boost for high speed chases – and for getting quickly under way in harbour. She was fitted with the latest air and surface warning radars, and electronic plotting facilities. *Devonshire's* complement consisted of thirty-three officers and over 400 ratings, and unlike in earlier warships, the accommodation was of a very high standard.

Another notable vessel built by Laird's in the immediate post war years was the Shaw Saville ship *Corinthic*, which was launched several months after *Ark Royal IV* had been laid down in the summer of 1946. She was a twin-screw vessel of 15,000 tons designed for the New Zealand passenger and freight carrying trade. The name of the ship was a departure from Shaw Saville's tradition of naming all their vessels after Maori tribes. When completed it was anticipated that she would make the long voyage out and back to New Zealand by any of three routes operated by the line, via Panama, Suez, or round the Cape of Good Hope. In her vast holds she had accommodation for 200,000 carcases of mutton or lamb or 400,000 boxes of butter in the refrigeration space. In addition to which she also had room for 4,000 tons of general cargo. As well as accommodation for once-living creatures she also had luxurious accommodation for eighty-five paying live human beings.

In common with other shipping companies, the Shaw Saville Line had suffered heavy losses during the war years, three of their fastest and latest motor cargo ships going down on the Malta convoy run in August 1942. In 1946, their plans to replace these losses were well in hand, for at that time they had in all four new vessels on order (including the *Corinthic*). An interesting fact related to the launch of this ship is that the naming ceremony was carried out by Mrs William Douglas, the daughter of the High Commissioner for New Zealand, the Hon. William Jordan. William Jordan had first made his way out to New Zealand in December 1904 on a Shaw Saville ship, bound for New

Destroyer Pearless

H.M. Submarine Sealion

H.M.S. Devonshire

Zealand with 500 other young men as a state-assisted emigrant. In his speech following the launch, which should have been conducted by his wife who was ill, Jordan said: "I'd like to meet my fellow passengers on that first trip, and I often wonder what they are doing now." One can though be fairly certain that few of them had managed to do as well as he obviously had!

Cammell Laird built its first ships for the Blue Star Line's South American trade in 1926 and 1927, the *Almeda Star*, the *Andalucia Star* and the *Arandora Star*. In 1948 they launched another ship for the line, the 10,723-ton *Uruguay Star*, one of four the firm built for the line, the other three being the *Paraguay Star*, *Argentina Star*, and the *Brazil Star*. The master appointed to command this ship was Captain G. Aldridge, who had been torpedoed twice during the war, in the *Andalucia Star* and the *Sultan Star*. The accommodation on this ship was extremely comfortable and could be compared with anything to be found in passenger liners. Many of the rooms had their own bathrooms. There was a dining saloon which was more like a very select West End restaurant, main lounge, and an excellent nursery for the children. The *Uruguay Star*, under Captain Aldridge, was essentially a happy ship, and this spirit infected all members of the crew. For the seamen the conditions were good. They were accommodated in cabins at the rate of just three or four to a room. They also had their own mess-deck and excellent catering facilities.

On April 14th 1950, Birkenhead's dock and shipyard workers watched with pride and interest as a sleek, grey and cream vessel slipped out of Victoria Dock into the Mersey. She was the *City of Birkenhead*. The first vessel to carry the Borough's name in that style was off on her maiden voyage to India, under the command of Captain Goring. She was to carry the town's name to many of the world's great ports, but she carried also the hallmark of fine craftsmanship, for the men who built her in Cammell Lairds yard. Built to carry 11,000 tons of cargo, the *City of Birkenhead* had cabin space for just four passengers in two magnificently-panelled state rooms, but on this her maiden voyage both were empty, perhaps an indication that the days of leisurely sea travel were at long last being superseded by air travel to distant lands. Birkenhead's association with this ship was marked by a plaque that was placed in the main dining room. Captain Goring was a native of Rochester on the Medway but her chief engineer was Mr Albert Davison, of Bebington.

During earlier years in Cammell Laird's history it was often said that Laird's yard without a warship was like a church without a congregation. During the 1950s the word "tanker" might easily have been added to this statement, for it seemed to be only on rare occasions that a slipway, a dry dock, or

Dunedin Star

the fitting basin was without one of these vessels. The funnel emblems of Esso, Shell, Eagle and BP became familiar sights in the yard. Among the ships that were built for these firms during this period were super tankers such as the *British Justice*, the *San Gerado*, and the *Zenatia*. The latter, built in 1957 for Shell Tankers Limited, was at the time, one of the two largest tankers to fly the Red Ensign with her displacement of 38,000 tons. As well as oil tankers Laird's was now to the fore in the production of other types of bulk carriers. In the year prior to the launch of the *Zenatia*, the firm had completed the 30,000-ton *Leader* for the Pan-Ore Steamship Company. At the time she was one of the largest ore carriers in the world.

Conventional ships were also built at the yard during the 1950s, two of these being the *Elizabeth Holt* and the *Florence Holt*, both being built to the order of the John Holt Line of Liverpool. Both ships were built for the west coast of Africa trade, and as not all of the ports of call in this part of the world were very attractive, particular attention had been paid to the layout of the officers' and crews' accommodation. The master, chief engineer and chief purser all had their own suites, and all other officers had single cabins with private w.c., washbasin and shower. In a far cry from the 'bad old days' for seamen and firemen, all the crewmen were berthed in the poop, with each man also having a single berth room. These rooms were also panelled in Gaboon plywood polished in the natural colour of the wood.

Laying the keel of a Blue Star vessel.

City of Birkenhead

1957 saw the launch of H.M.S. *Grampus*, the first post-war submarine to be launched at the yard. The summer of this year also saw the start of work on the building of two new graving docks at the yard with the clearance of land forming part of the ancient churchyard of St. Mary's. Into this land the proposed dry dock was to be extended. Both docks were part of the company's £17 million reconstruction and modernisation programme intended to put the Birkenhead yard in an advantageous position for the construction of the larger tankers now being ordered and to counter foreign competition. Existing facilities at the time permitted the building of vessels up to 70,000 tons, but the clear indication was that greater capacity would be required in the near future.

December 1957 saw the commissioning of H.M.S. *Tenby* at Birkenhead, the 256th ship which Messrs Cammell Laird had built for the Royal Navy. *Tenby* was an anti-submarine frigate and was a sister ship to H.M.S. *Whitby* which had been built at the yard and commissioned in July 1956. This month saw the laying of the keel of the 38,000-ton passenger liner *Windsor Castle*, for the Union Castle Mail Steamship Company. She was to be the first big passenger liner to be built at the yard since the Cunard liner *Mauretania* had been launched there in June 1939. All in all this was a notable month for the firm for it also saw the launch of the 18,000-ton tanker *Lucellum* for H.E. Moss & Company, the launch of a 10,750-ton motor cargo liner for clients of S.G. Embincos Ltd, and of a tug for North West Tugs Ltd.

In 1958 the firm made yet another notable contribution to the famous Shaw Saville Fleet by completing the refrigerated cargo liner *Ionic* for the Line. The *Ionic* was the twentieth vessel built for the line by Laird's since the Second World War, and was the third Shaw Saville ship to bear this name. Old people on Merseyside today will remember the second *Ionic*, a very famous passenger and cargo carrier which performed sterling service as a transport in the 1914-18 War, and was sold for breaking up after years of almost unbroken service in the U.K./New Zealand trade.

The *Ionic* was ship No. 1281, which was followed by a 4,044-ton cargo vessel, the *Alice Bowater*, built for the Bowater Steamship Company. The locally-based Bibby Bros. Ltd were responsible for the next vessel which was a Doxford engined cargo ship of 7,201 tons, the keel of which was laid on July 22nd 1958. She was named the *Cheshire*. More orders were then in hand from the Admiralty, the Guided Missile Destroyer H.M.S. *Devonshire* being built at the yard during 1958 and 1959, which was followed by the building of the frigate H.M.S. *Ajax*. Vessel No. 1286 was the *Crystal*

The 1588 ton turret vessel Los Andes, launched on 29th October 1874.

The 524 ton twin screw vessel H.M.S. Rattlesnake, launched on 11th September 1886.

Windsor Castle

Sapphire, a 10,295-ton cargo liner built for the Sugar Line. It was vessel No. 1287 which was, once again, to make shipbuilding history on Merseyside, the afore-mentioned passenger and cargo liner *Windsor Castle*.

For some time now the Cammell Laird shipyard had been the scene of long on-going industrial action, all of which was related to whether boilermakers or shipwrights should chalk lines on the ships' plates. In all, this had involved 1,750 men. They returned to work though, after a long and bitter dispute on June 23rd 1959, and were then soon among a crowd of 50,000 people who had arrived at the yard to watch the launch of the 37,639-ton Union Castle liner *Windsor Castle*.

On this notable day, strike-hit Cammell Lairds produced a lock-out of a different kind ... for hundreds of ticket-holders trying to get into the yard to see the Queen Mother launch the liner. There were angry scenes at the entrance as ticket-holders hammered on locked gates, and argued with police and officials. The cause of all this distress was due to the fact that most of the ticket-holders should have been in position at 12.30, over half-an-hour before the time of the launching, but were delayed by huge traffic jams converging on the yard. So many were trying to force their way into the yard that those in charge felt that they dared not risk opening the gates to let the delayed guests in. The launch itself though was performed in brilliant sunshine, to the cheers of the thousands present. The R.M.S. *Windsor Castle* was the largest ship of her kind to have been built in Britain since the war – and the largest ever to be built in an English shipyard. She was designed to clip time off the Royal Mail route to South Africa, and at the same time carry her many passengers in elegant and luxurious accommodation. Her two-shaft machinery installation with a total shaft horse-power of 45,000 was the largest ever put in such a merchant ship.

If records had been broken by the building of the *Windsor Castle*, more were soon to be broken by the building and launching of the 65,500-ton Royal Dutch Shell Tanker *Sepia*. This ship, which had an overall length of 817 feet, was the biggest tanker and the biggest merchant ship the firm had built. This vessel was the first tanker Laird's had built for Shell Tankers M.V. of Rotterdam, but the twelfth tanker for Shell since they had started building for them some twenty-four years previous to this launch. Her launch, on February 18th 1961, attracted a large crowd. The *Sepia* was the second of her name to be launched by Shell, the first being a 9,000-tonner launched in 1906. After an honourable and long life, this ship was sold for scrap just over twelve months before Laird's launched *Sepia II*.

In 1962 the 2,725-ton passenger vessel *Manx Maid* was completed for the Isle of Man Steam Packet Company Ltd. She was the first car ferry built for these owners, and also the first vessel on the Isle of Man service to be fitted with stabilisers. She had a special system of ramps to facilitate the embarkation and disembarkation of vehicles at Douglas, Isle of Man, at any state of the tide.

Another Laird-built ferry also went into service in 1962, this being the Birkenhead Corporation vessel *Overchurch*. Designed to clip two minutes off the run across the Mersey to Liverpool, she had several features which distinguished her from the older Mersey ferry boats *Mountwood* and *Woodchurch*, the *Overchurch* having a totally-enclosed bridge, with wide visibility windows, stretching across the full beam of the ship. The windows of the saloons were also longer than in the other two ferry boats and passengers could therefore sit and enjoy a panoramic view of the Mersey.

The top deck of the *Overchurch* had a large shelter at the forward end, arranged with seats, but most of this deck was set aside as a promenade area. At the aft end of the main deck was a covered space set aside for stowing cycles. The passenger accommodation on the lower deck consisted of a saloon on the forward side of the machinery space fitted with upholstered seats, and a tea bar at the forward end – a feature which was found to be most welcome by weary commuters.

Among the ships completed at the yard in 1962 was a most unusual one, namely the Country's fastest cable ship, the 8,961-ton C.S. *Mercury*. Launched on July 20th 1962, she was built for Cable & Wireless Ltd., the international communications group. The *Mercury* was a remarkable ship in that she had a hull strengthened for operating in ice, with internal air conditioning of a very sophisticated type which, with her heating arrangements, allowed her to work efficiently in both tropical waters and temperatures as low as zero degrees Farenheit. An unusual feature of the ship was that she had twin funnels abreast, enabling her upper deck to be devoted almost entirely to cable work. Living and storeroom space were restricted to the decks above and below. This arrangement left the cable deck clear, and enclosed, so that work could be carried on under any climatic conditions. Fresh water could be made on board, at a cost, in 1962, of one shilling and nine pence a ton, by the use of a completely novel method of evaporation. This installation made her completely independent of external water supplies.

The first master of the *Mercury* was Captain C.H.C. Reynolds, a Fishguard man. The ship's first

Samaria

cable-laying task was to lay two-fifths of the 8,000-mile telephone cable linking Australia and New Zealand with Vancouver. When fully loaded *Mercury* could carry 1,200 miles of deep-sea cable and forty-eight submersible repeaters. To lay the 3,200 miles of cable needed involved her in three round trips from London to the Pacific, a total voyaging distance of some 60,000 miles. The diesel electric propelled *Mercury* was 470 feet long and had a maximum speed of 16 knots. She carried a complement of 135 officers and men, the majority of her crew in 1962 being Spanish. Two years later the firm completed another ship for Cable and Wireless, the cable repair vessel *Cable Enterprise* – a smaller ship than the *Mercury* at just 4,358 tons.

October 1964 found Mr Robert Johnson, the progressive young chairman of the company in the thirteenth century port of Bergen, where he entertained fifty shipowners from the port. He explained to his influential guests that British shipbuilding was in the doldrums, but he was determined to go out personally to sell Cammell Laird's excellent products. What he was selling in fact was the innovative concept of offering, in a well-illustrated catalogue, six standard ship designs for sale on an "off-the-peg" basis! The vessels on offer comprised three cargo ships, two bulk carriers and a tanker, varying in tonnage from 3,150 tons to 57,400 deadweight, with speeds varying from 14 to 17 knots.

Mr Johnson went on to explain that Cammell Lairds had modernised its yard at a cost of £8 million, and over the next five years intended to spend another £8 million on improvements, which he firmly believed was the biggest step taken in the history of British shipbuilding. All of which was being done to attract overseas trade. He continued by explaining that the cost of Laird "standard ships" would be considerably lower than "tailor-made" ones – and he (courageously?) stated he could give firm delivery dates. He concluded this hard sell by assuring his Norwegian guests that his company would give long-term credits, and would even accept payment on semi-barter terms – if the commodity offered was acceptable! As one reporter present at this gathering put it, "I left Mr Johnson with the impression that the first owner to place an order will get it at 'bargain basement' prices." Alas though, it had been forty-four years since Cammell Lairds had built for a Norwegian owner, but pending charter arrangements at least were some indication that Mr Johnson's spirited efforts had been worthwhile.

The recently-established Cunard-Laird Joint Venture was further developed in October 1964 with the launch of the third ship to bear the name *Samaria*. This 7,500-ton cargo liner was planned to go into operation on Cunard's London-New York-Philadelphia service early in 1975. Launched by Lady Benson, wife of Sir Henry Benson, the *Samaria* was built to operate with her Cammell Laird built sister ship, *Scythia* in maintaining a fortnightly service across the Atlantic. The interesting thing about this venture was that both ships were not owned by Cunard but by the North West Line (Mersey) Ltd, a member of the Cammell Laird Group, and were merely to be placed on long-term charter to Cunard. A third vessel, the 40,787-ton bulk carrier *Siglion* was, at this time, also on order to the M.W. Line, but she was soon to be handed over to her Norwegian charterers – Sigval Bergesen, of Oslo!

The *Samaria*, *Scythia* and the *Siglion* were all planned to play an important role in Cunard's plans at this time to further develop their 'new-look' cargo fleet on the North Atlantic, together with the four new ships, *Media*, *Parthia*, *Saxonia* and *Ivernia* – recently placed on the Liverpool-New York cargo service. The use of the name *Samaria* by Cunard revived one of their famous fleet names, the first *Samaria* of 2,574 tons gross, having been built in 1868. The *Samaria II* was a 21,000-ton passenger liner which went into service in 1922 on the run from Liverpool to New York, which, as already noted, was also built at Lairds. It was therefore a nice gesture on Cunard's part to use this name once more on another of their Laird-built ships.

Further developments of a co-operative nature took place in 1967 with the establishment of the *Dorchester Club* – an international association of five major European shipbuilders. This venture was founded to pool the extensive design and production experience of the members: Cammell Laird Shipbuilders Ltd., England; Aktien-Gesellschaft "Wesser", Germany; Rijn-Scheide-Veroime, Holland; Italcantiera, Spain; and Cantoeri Navali Riuniti, Italy.

On June 25th 1964, the keel of H.M.S. *Renown* was laid, this being vessel No. 1316. The 425 foot long submarine was the first nuclear-powered vessel to be built in the yard. She was the first of three such ships to be built by the company, the other two being H.M.S. *Revenge* and H.M.S. *Conqueror*. The first two of this trio were nuclear powered strategic missile carrying submarines, whereas H.M.S. *Conqueror* is a hunter-killer submarine not capable of carrying strategic missiles. She was in fact the submarine that sank the Argentinian warship 'Belgrano' with conventional torpedoes during

H.M.S. *Conqueror*

the Falklands conflict. As the first of these ships were capable of carrying strategic missiles their construction proved as controversial in this century as the construction of the *Alabama* had in the last.

While the controversial nuclear submarine programme gained momentum, the yard continued to find a variety of other work. In June 1966 the firm secured a rather novel order, for the construction of the bare hull of a 46,000-ton d.w. bulk carrier for Furness Shipbuilding Ltd., of Haverton Hill-on-Tees. This was the second time in five years that Lairds had taken an order for the construction of a ship's hull only, the other being for Kristiansands Mek Verk.

In May 1966 the Company handed over the twin-screw steamer *Ben-my-Chree* to the Isle of Man Steam Packet Company, the 14th vessel to be built by Lairds for this firm. In addition to her compliment of 1,400 passengers, *Ben-my-Chree* was designed to carry up to seventy cars. A vessel of 2,762 tons, she had a service speed of 21 knots. As in the *Manx Maid*, the loading and unloading of cars was by way of a spiral arrangement of ramps at the after end of the ship which enabled vehicles to be driven on and off irrespective of the state of the tide at Douglas, where there is an unusually large tide range. Of great interest to those that suffer from sea-sickness was the fact that *Ben-my-Chree* had been fitted with stabilisers, and particular attention had been paid to ventilation of the passenger accommodation. Four of her decks were at the disposal of her passengers. Of interest to those that had to navigate her was the fact that she was fitted with a bow rudder.

During 1970 Cammell Laird & Company (Shipbuilders & Engineers) Ltd., ceased to be a wholly-owned subsidiary of Cammell Laird & Company Ltd. (now the Laird Group). The ownership of the ordinary stock of the Company became vested in the Public Trustee and the Laird Group in equal proportions. The new Apprentice Training Centre also started to operate in this year, which was considered at the time to be one of the finest of its kind in the country. The purpose of this facility was to give classroom training to the first year apprentices. It had a capacity to deal with 290 youngsters.

1970 also saw the launch of the Canadian Pacific vessel *Voyageur*, a 15,680-ton container ship built for this line by Lairds as one of three sister ships, the other identical vessels being the *Adventurer* and the *Discoverer*, all of which were designed to travel at 17.75 knots. The following year saw the

59

Ben-my-Chree

launch of the 22,800-ton liquid petroleum gas/ammonia carrier *Gazana* – the first vessel of this highly specialized type to be built in the shipyard. She was one of two similar ships, the other being the *Gambada*, both of which were built for the Peninsular & Oriental Steam Navigation Company.

In 1972 the 20,059-ton bulk carrier *Oakworth* was launched, which vessel had been built for the Watergate Ship Company. She was designed to travel with her heavy load at 15.8 knots. Another interesting batch of orders was also dealt with in 1972. These were for three indentical vessels built to the order of the Royal Mail Lines. They were the 12,320-ton general cargo ships *Orbita*, *Orduna* and *Ortega*, all of them having a service speed of 17.25 knots.

It was also in 1972 that the Government announced its intentions to provide the finance for a substantial programme of modernisation for the shipyard – the most extensive project of its kind ever undertaken by the Company. The final phase – the building of a vast covered construction hall – was to be completed in 1978. Monday, September 25th 1972, marked the introduction of a change of name and the adoption of a new "visual image" for the Company.

The name was shortened to Cammell Laird Shipbuilders Ltd and the old emblem of the camel, used since 1903, was replaced with a new logo. This was a monogram with the letters CL in red on a white background, the letters being formed from the main features of a ship – the bow, the stern and the funnel.

In 1974 the car-passenger ferry *St. Edmund* was completed for Sealink. A ship of 9,000 tons gross, she was the flagship of the Sealink fleet and considered at the time to be the best passenger-car ferry ever built by Cammell Lairds. She was for service on the Sealink run between Harwich and the Hook of Holland. The following year saw the completion of a most unusual vessel at the yard, a canal narrow boat. It was followed by the building of more of these craft for use by handicapped children.- These vessels, though, were not built by the main yard but designed and built exclusively by the first-year apprentices in the aforementioned training facility, all of which allowed them to gain practical experience in actual ship construction.

In 1975 the first of four standard petroleum tankers known as StaT 32 (Standard Tanker 32,000 tonnes) was launched. All four tankers were subsequently acquired by the Royal Fleet Auxilliary

Service and three were then converted to "Replenish at Sea Tankers". All were to see service in the Falklands campaign. The following year found the yard busy working on the first of three Type 42 guided missile destroyers, under construction for the Royal Navy, the first of which, H.M.S. *Birmingham*, was commissioned in 1976. In 1977 the M.V. *Algol*, the first of seven standard petroleum tankers known as StaT 55 (Standard Tanker 55,000 tonnes) was completed for Algol Shipping, a member of the Vlasov Group.

During 1977 Cammell Laird Shipbuilders Ltd. became a member of British Shipbuilders, a new corporation set up to run the nationalised shipbuilding industry. Vesting day was July 1st when thirty companies engaged in shipbuilding, marine engine building, and ship repairing, together with more than ninety associated concerns, became members of British Shipbuilders. Subsequent to this development, in 1978 the yard celebrated 150 years of shipbuilding in Birkenhead, which event was made notable by the opening of the giant new covered construction hall, a £32 million "ship factory" the funding for which had been provided by the Government. This new facility brought indoor working conditions to the yard, not for the first time, but for the first time on such a grand scale. The idea behind this development was that it would mark the end of shipbuilding under "building site" conditions, and greatly reduce wasted time due to bad weather. This huge building now dominates the waterfront at Birkenhead. The size of it can be gleaned from the fact that it is capable of containing ships of up to 120,000 tons and of producing five or six 50,000-ton ships a year – given the orders. H.M.S. *Edinburgh* was the second guided missile destroyer to be built under cover in this new construction hall by what is known as the "Open Ship" method. The ship, complete with main engines, gearing, propeller and shafting, and most of her internal fitting being worked on in the hall and then extruded a few feet at a time onto the conventional outside slipway ready for launching.

The 1980s saw the Company move into the construction of exploration drilling rigs for the oil industry. The keel of the first of these, the 18,708-ton *Sovereign Explorer* was laid on November 24th 1981, the rig eventually being handed over on July 25th 1985. This complex vessel was built on the "GVA 4000" design adapted for drilling in water of up to 600 metres. Two Azimuth Thrusters assist positioning and afford a 6 knot transit speed. She was built for the owners Lombard Leasings Ltd., in conjunction with Dome Petroleums, and was designed by Messrs Gotaverken Arendal (GVA).

The yard's existence as a nationalised part of British Shipbuilders did not last for long. In June 1985 the Company came out of the public sector, joining V.S.E.L. in Barrow under the corporate heading V.S.E.L. Consortium PLC.

Another offshore oil industry vessel produced by the yard in 1985 was a self-elevating accommodation

Sovereign Explorer

platform. This unit has a rectangular pontoon hull with six tiers of superstructure dedicated to workforce accommodation. Four 87.7m legs with hydraulic jacking systems enable the unit to operate in tidal waters to a maximum depth of 47.5m. Facilities include deck storage areas, storerooms, workshops, cinema and a gymnasium, a crawler crane with maximum capacity of 50 tonnes and a maximum radius of 50 metres affording payload handling. A helideck suitable for Sikorsky helicopters is located to the side of the main structure. The designers of this unit were Messrs Marine Structure Consultants (MSC) b.v.

Also building at the yard in 1985 was the type 22, batch 3 frigate H.M.S. *Campbeltown*. She is an all-gas turbine twin-screw anti-submarine vessel powered by an arrangement of two Rolls Royce Spey Gas Turbines of 37,540 horse-power, and two Rolls Royce Tyne Gas Turbines of 8,500 horse-power. In March 1989 she was handed over to the Royal Navy at Devonport, having been built in record time by the highly-skilled Birkenhead workforce. When these words were written it was reported that she was doing well on her trials! H.M.S. *Campbeltown* was not the first Royal Navy vessel to bear this name, *Campbeltown I* being one of a batch of fifty United States destroyers transferred to the Royal Navy in the Second World War. She was, however, to be the first Royal Navy ship of this name to be built in the United Kingdom.

Campbeltown I, it will be remembered, played a major role in the historic raid on St. Nazaire, when she rammed the dock gates of this port, thus preventing the dry-docking of German warships such as the *Scharnhorst* and the *Tirpitz*. As she hurtled towards these gates at full speed the crew had to jump for their lives. A day later the ship destroyed the lock entirely by blowing itself up. The ship's commander at this time, Lieutenant Commander S. Beattie, was awarded the VC for this action.

At the conclusion of this long story about the famous shipbuilding yard established at Birkenhead by William Laird in 1829, the firm, in March 1989 – 160 years later, was engaged on the construction of three conventional diesel submarines, the latest of which is H.M.S. *Unseen*. All of these vessels have a displacement of 2,400 tons and will be manned by a crew of forty-four. Their armaments consist of 6 x 21" torpedo tubes with 12 re-load. Surface speed is be 12 knots with a diving speed of 20 knots, and all three ships have a range of 8,000 miles.

Looking back on the long history of this world-famous enterprise, as mentioned in Chapter 1, the first real vessel to be built at Birkenhead by William Laird was the 148-ton paddle steamer *Lady Lansdowne*, built, paradoxically, to alleviate unemployment in Ireland in the 1830s. Today, as I write in the summer of 1991, uncertainty over the yard's future, and the related prospect of unemployment, hangs like a spectre over the great shipbuilding town of Birkenhead. All of us on Merseyside are of the opinion that this yard should remain open for the construction of ships for many years to come. If it does (and we are of the opinion that it must, not merely for the sake of Merseyside, but in order to see that Britain retains a realistic shipbuilding capability), then one can be confident that the skilled men of Cammell Laird's will continue to produce great ships.

The welded steamer, Fullagar, launched on 2nd May 1920.

BIBLIOGRAPHY

Primary Sources

Files CL 2 – CL 20 Held at the Williamson Art Gallery & Museum, Birkenhead. Also:– File 291, 321, 775, 797, 803, 1028, 1029, Laird Family File. The origins of the Laird Family in the parish of Kilmalcolm.

A list of ships built at Cammell Lairds, 1956-1984 – Cammell Laird Shipbuilders Ltd.

Memorandum by N. F. Cave – Cammell Laird & Co. – on Huascar, 13th July 1970.

Laird Brothers of Birkenhead – List of ships built 1829-1943.

The Laird Family Papers – held by Marianne M. Laird, Hereford.

A Family Memoir by Eleanor Bristow Laird, 1904(Ms).

Our Story – Cammell Laird & Company.

Portraits – Autobiographic Sketches of The Six – On William Laird, published by Messrs Wilmers, Birkenhead, 1888.

Expedition into the interior of Africa by Macgregor Laird and R. A. K. Oldfield, 1830.

Lairds Magazine, 1957-1960.

The Shipping World, 25th March 1953.

Post & Mercury, May 23rd 1918.

Illustrated London News, July 27th 1861.

The Porcupine, September 26th 1868.

The Liverpool Courier, January 27th 1893.

Fairplay, September 8th 1921, 26th June 1947.

Syren & Shipping, 25th June 1947.

Our Fleet Today by Captain Seardley-Wilmot R.N., published 1900.

The Practical Magazine No. 18, Volume 3, 1874.

Ark Royal, issued for the Admiralty by The Ministry of Information, 1942.

'On Mr Laird and The Alabama', *The Liverpool Mercury*, July 1865.

Liverpool Post & Mercury, July 11th 1832, December 18th 1925.

The Annals of Liverpool – from *Gores Directory*, 1895.

The Illustrated London News, September 17th 1870.

The Annals of Birkenhead – from *Wards Directory of Birkenhead*, 1857.

The Elder Dempster Line – House Magazine, December 1931.

Numerous articles from the local press obtained from Birkenhead Central Library – over 50 in all.

'Shipbuilders of Merseyside', *Journal of Commerce*, 19th February 1944.

Secondary Sources

Our First 150 years, published by Cammell Laird Shipbuilders Ltd.

Builders of Great Ships, published by Cammell Laird & Company (Shipbuilders & Engineers) Ltd.

Shipbuilders to the World, published by Cammell Laird Shipbuilders Ltd.

The History of Cammell Laird, published by Cammell Laird Shipbuilders Ltd.

Cammell Laird and the Royal Navy, published Cammell Laird & Co. Ltd, 1960.

Against the King's Enemies. The story of Cammell Laird-built Warships, published Cammell Laird & Co.

Branigan, Denis, *John Laird: Iron Shipbuilder*.

Budlong Tyler, David, *Steam, Conquers the Atlantic*, published by D. Appleton-Century Co., 1939.

Davies, Dr P.H., *An expedition to identify and survey the wreck of the paddle steamer Lady Lansdowne'*.

Haram, ?, *Ancient History & Present Conditions of Birkenhead*, 1844.

Jamieson, William, *Ark Royal*, published by Rupert Hart Davis, 1957.

Jellicoe, Admiral Viscount, of Scapa, *The Grand Fleet, 1914-1916*.

Lennox Kerr, J., *The Unfortunate Ship – the story of H.M. Troopship Birkenhead*.

Lubbock, Basil, *The China Clippers*, published James Brown & Son, Glasgow 1916.

Macy, Jesse, *The Anti-Slavery Crusade*, published by Yale University Press, 1919.

Miller, A. H., *Cregaragh* – on the sons of Rob Roy.

Scott, Sir Walter, *Rob Roy*, published by Thomas Nelson & Sons, 1901.

Semmes, R., *The Confederate Raider, Alabama*.

Sulley, Phillip, F.R.H.S., *The History of Birkenhead*, 1907.

Underhill, Harold A., *Sail Training & Cadet Ships*, published by Brown Son & Ferguson, 1956.

'The River Niger – Macgregor Laird and those who inspired him', *Journal of the African Society*, Volume XXX1, October 1932.

'A West African Centenary – Macgregor Laird's expeditions', *The Times*, January 27th 1932.

The Directory of National Biography – John Laird 1805-1874 and Macgregor Laird 1808-1861.

Birkenhead 60 years ago – Birkenhead & Cheshire Advertiser, Jubilee Souvenir, 1913.

West African Review, July 1932.

The 3434 ton screw steamer Puno, launched on 3rd March 1873.